MONEY WITH BENEFITS

(A Unique Financing Weapon)

> *"It's like growing Money on steroids "*

Samuel J. Augustine

Whenever people gather and start discussing money, it inevitably turns into a conversation about investing and Rates of Return. That's a recipe for disaster.

A Promise for You

Those reading and practicing this Method

Will come out

Better Off Financially

Than those focused on Rates of Return

It's that Inevitable

OTHER BOOKS BY AUTHOR

THEY WENT IN HARM'S WAY

DEDICATION

FOR THE BENEFIT OF
THOSE READING THESE PAGES

This publication is designed to provide accurate and authoritative information in regard to the subject matter covered. It is sold with the understanding that the publisher is not engaged in rendering legal, or other professional services. If legal or other professional assistance is required, the services of such a person should be sought.

Contents

AUTHOR'S PREFACE

Having lunch with a top executive at one of the largest casinos in our nation. I was curious and thought to ask him how much revenue flowed through the casino yearly. I had an idea from published information I read previously on the Internet and the numbers were consistent with those he gave me.

With the sound of a few thousand slot machines for background music, and regardless if you read it or you hear it, knowing that the casino will have revenues pushing a billion dollars annually in the not too distant future, well, it's a large number to grasp.

I looked at my friend who by the way towered over me. He is the epitome of the 'gentle giant.' When you first meet him, you don't expect to feel the warmth and love he shares for everybody. Quite the opposite! My first impression of Ron Davis found him to be very intimidating. However, he quickly helps you overcome those fears. Besides being a former NFL defensive end, Ron is well known locally and has earned respect for his help in and outside of our community. He is actively involved in many local charities and projects. In addition to the time he puts into his work, Ron has been committed to the NFL players union, making him one very busy guy.

When he answered my question, I came back with a wise guy remark. Can't help myself, I guess I enjoy having others hear what I'm thinking, even if they prefer not to know. "Why not install drive-in windows?" During the brief pause that followed, he simply gave me a stern look, shook his head, and smiled. His smile was like a green light for me, so I went on, "That way people can just drive up to the window and hand you their money." Again, he just shook his head and smiled. Yes, I was pleased it didn't go any further.

It is so easy to forget that gambling is a form of entertainment, not a method to add funds to a retirement account. I won't question it can be exciting to hear the slot machines ringing with the sounds of a winner, or pass a card game where the intensity is as strong as it is for one intensely watching a professional championship event. Remember, this is a fun way to entertain yourself.

Some people want extra money to purchase extravagant items. Others want money just to put food on the table for their family. It is an unusual person who to some degree, doesn't desire more money than they already have.

My comment suggesting that casino's use drive-up windows to make it easier for people to drop off their money caused me to put my thinking cap on. It seems that's just what we do with our money, we literally give it away. I'm not talking about a few dollars lost in a casino either. Every one of us give hundreds of thousands of dollars away during our lifetimes and we don't think twice about it. Once again, I'm emphasizing that's hundreds of thousands of dollars.

Compared to how most of us throw money away without thinking about it, I would offer that gambling, when constrained, may be the only enjoyable way to do it.

Another view to avoid squandering our money, offered from almost everyone is to learn how to budget. Well, to a point, I can agree. Yet, so often I have watched as people went on a budget, and while a few succeeded, most didn't. It goes against our personal culture. We are human beings and our behavior is typically set by the time we reach our early twenties. According to behavioral scientists, it's difficult to change who and what we are beyond that stage in life.

This isn't about investment ideas either. On occasion, you might be among a group of friends and find yourself talking about investments. Someone will bring up their retirement plan at work. Others may even add savings and brokerage accounts to the total. Then someone brings up his or her Rate of Return on their portfolio. The conversation turns in this direction and no one understands or appreciates they are courting disaster.

This is about the money you throw away. It's not about what you buy whether it's to fill a need or a pleasure. It's about the bills you pay every month and the part we shouldn't ever pay. It's how you dissect those bills and one problem is that so few of us do. We get a bill in the mail and we send in a check or, in today's world, we have the bank pay the bill from our account, in which case many never open the envelope and look at the actual payment notice. Instead, we glance at the total due.

Many people are careful to try and make purchases at what they believe is the lowest cost possible. We look for discounts on items we want and finding the right discount, we purchase the product. Yet, we fail to see that many of our purchases, even the discounted ones, may actually cost up to twice what we think we paid for them. This reflects on the idea of buying something and then unthinkingly we give the seller more just for the privilege of allowing us to make the purchase. Unbelievable!

For instance, you may be considering a large purchase. You think to yourself whether you should pay cash or use credit. You really don't know the best method and both of these methods are available to you.

Would it surprise you to discover that both ways are more than likely wrong? There is actually another, relatively unknown way to get that car and the only one that even needs to know how you did it, is you. This concept is so simple; you'll ask yourself why hasn't anyone has ever shown you this before.

Once upon a time, I heard what was supposed to be a joke.

"Why don't cows have any money, because farmers milk them dry."

Sadly, it is no longer a joke. Now, watch as that is played out!

On April 2, 2018 I read an article in the NY Post centered on credit cards. I was amazed to see that the median credit card balance was $15,983 and the average interest charge on an account is 18.6%

I found that hard to swallow so I went to work on this problem. I suspected that I already knew the answer, but wanted to verify it. You can see what others and I have known for decades.

In this example, I decided to have our credit card holder pay just the credit card interest of $247 per month, check out the results, quite the difference,

Card Supplier	Credit Card	My Method
Starting Debt	$ 16,000	$ 16,000
Monthly Payments	$ 247/month	$ 225/month
Balance in 7 years	$ 16,000	$ -0-

Doing it using a proven method over two centuries, both the interest and the balance are paid off. Whereas, paying the credit card company just the interest doesn't benefit you at all.

Additionally, the method I'm sharing with you has another benefit. The outcome of which deposits $5,000 into your savings account. It's your money, it's not a gift, and it's in the contract. The $16,000 debt you paid off is coming back to you. Yes, that's more than $21,000 and it's your money, in your account, in your name.

Another view, for our example, might be someone who decides to pay off the credit card in seven years, that's in 84 months. The payment required to pay it off would be $342 every month. Using my method, this also provides an extraordinary result. Doing it the way I am proposing, paying the same $342 every month results in paying the debt off after only 54 months.

Again, using the same starting point we get,

Card Supplier	Credit Card	My Method
Starting Debt	$ 16,000	$ 16,000
Payments	$ 342/month	$ 342/month
Debt paid-off in	84 months	54 months
Total Payments	$ 28,722	$ 17,901
Payment Savings		**$ 10,821**

This is not a trick. It is not switching credit cards. It's a simple strategy that works for you and your family. It can work fast and it can be repeatedly used during your entire lifetime. Once the plan is put in motion, you own it, you control it. Your days as a cow are over.

Isn't that great? As you will see, people have been doing this for nearly two hundred years including some very famous names you will have no problem recognizing. Once again, you are making money. Paying the bill quicker not only saves $10,821 in out of pocket payments, but leaves you with the same $21,000 cash from the first example. In this scenario by setting aside the additional monthly savings, you will be ahead by about $32,000. That's $32,000, that's your money. You won't lose it to the finance companies or to the banks.

Oops, I almost forgot, there's another important advantage to this methodology. Your credit score will improve rapidly once this system is in place. In case you are wondering how important that is, go ask any mortgage broker or bank lending officer.

We don't have to change our spending habits. We just have to make an adjustment in the financing methods we use. We have to shed some popular and foolish clichés to accomplish this, but an open mind will recognize and welcome this procedure. Using this system creates wealth for anyone smart enough to utilize it.

There are some who believe we should save up the money needed and pay cash for larger purchases. Surprisingly, this can be a major trap for those who do. They lose many times more money than what they saved and they never know it. In the end, as you will learn, they are no better off than the borrower.

Think about that because next time you go to pay for a vacation or put a new roof on your home, whether you finance it or pay cash, this principle applies to you. Yes, how you pay for any large purchase has a dramatic effect on your bottom line, and most people are blatantly unaware of this.

My goals include helping you by demonstrating how you can keep more money in your own pockets, provide large amounts of liquidity, and bring a higher level of security to your family while enjoying more of the things that life has to offer. I intend to demonstrate still one more large benefit. This concept can noticeably add supplemental income in your retirement years as well.

From years of experience, five decades to be exact of personal experience as well as that drawn from others in my profession, that this concept of money remains somewhat of a secret. Not from lack of it being shared, but because of previous misconceptions, people don't want to hear about it. Even for those who may have happily used it from time to time, most never fully understood how it works.

I can't claim to be among the first sharing these ideas, especially since I learned the basics from others as far back as 1969. Although back then, when I began helping people purchase this program, I was the one who took decades to appreciate the benefits. I didn't fully comprehend the very product that I used to assist people. Looking back, I have only myself to blame.

It came as a surprise to discover recently, that there are some professionals expanding these concepts well beyond where I had gone. This has been a pleasant and inspiring revelation.

It doesn't matter if you are just starting out in life, the CEO of a large company, or you are retired. The ideas inside these pages can be extremely profitable for you. The rewards are here for you, your family, and for future generations.

I believe that once you have read and put this information to use, you will be a new person, wiser and smarter in basic financial matters then many self-proclaimed investment intellectuals, including many with initials after their names. There are few if any, better ideas than those found inside these pages.

I haven't forgotten about those casinos. Using my method, you will feel better when you put coins in those slot machines, because these will be discretionary dollars you are using, not dollars you may depend upon.

Ron Davis shared an important feeling he has about the decisions we face and how they can affect our lives. "People are afraid to open doors when they don't know what's on the other side, but I look at that as an opportunity."

If I had one wish today as I look back, it would be that I understood how to use this product much earlier in my life. In today's world, younger people want to enjoy life and still put away money. In your sunset years, you may want to enjoy life with more discretionary dollars.

Younger people can literally save hundreds of thousands of dollars by following the path I am laying out. It doesn't require in most cases a change of lifestyle. An older person can enjoy a richer, fuller 'economic' lifestyle by increasing cash flow through the knowledge and utilization of the options available to them.

As of the end of 2018, there was $944 billion dollars in total credit card debt. Add to that student loans, car loans, personal bank loans, store loans and various other debts, this is a time of urgency for those businesses and people that want to control their destinies.

To everyone reading these pages, I sincerely pray that what you learn will be financially beneficial to you all.

Chapter 1

The Way We Are

> "Status Quo you know, is Latin for
> The mess we're in"
> Ronald Reagan

One day, many years ago, one of my seven daughters walked into my office. Among her duties, was the responsibility to maintain our business books and pay bills. She did the day to day in-house accounting for our small firm.

Then it happened on a Tuesday morning. She sat down in front of me and her body language told me that whatever she had to say, it was important. I immediately stopped what I was doing. I sat back and looked at her. I'll never forget what happened next as she began talking.

She said, "We've run out of money for the month." Because we always work using current cash flow which is sufficient to handle our monthly expenses, her announcement startled me. We have a rule, which simply is that once money came out of the business, it stayed out. I asked her, "How short are we, how did this happen?" She sort of gulped and said, "About $30,000." I was glad she gulped, because I did too. She went on to explain how our cash flow was low for a couple of months and that we would be up to speed the following month.

I remember this scene well. I looked at her, thought about it for a moment, and finally said I would give her a check in two days to cover the $30,000. Then on Thursday morning after checking with the bank and assuring myself that the money was now sitting in my personal checking account, I called my daughter into my office. It was around eleven o'clock, I handed her the check I promised just two days earlier. She said, "Thank you" and disappeared.

The day was going smooth when after a few hours she came back into my office. Again, she sat down in front of me. She informed me that she paid the remaining bills. Yet, she had this familiar troubled look, and I began thinking to myself, "Here we go again." I said, "That's good, so why do you still look so concerned?"

She came back at me, "Ok dad, I've checked every one of your accounts, investments and banking. I can't find where you got it. How did you suddenly get the $30,000?" she asked in an almost demanding way. Wow, I was startled, her tone sounded accusatory. Still, I managed a smile and explained the method I used.

I thought to myself that it was strange that she struggled with the information I gave her. She is an Investment Advisor, and a good one. Yet, she is hardly alone. I thought to myself that too many Advisors are grossly unfamiliar with this concept.

One of the major obstacles for people to acquire financial success, is the sudden need for cash. It comes in many forms. It could be the need for another car, a new refrigerator, or to repair a wall where you notice water dripping from what is now the need for a new roof. The repeated uses for using savings are wealth killers.

Typically, when there are needs for larger amounts of cash, some people will go to their bank to make a personal loan. We've all been there. We go into the bank, fill out a dozen pieces of paper work, and wait anxiously for the bank's decision.

In another scenario, with sufficient amounts available on credit cards, some will use it knowing they are reducing their available credit on their cards. They fail to recognize that they have borrowed money, just as if it came from the bank, but at a much higher rate of interest.

The great comedian Bob Hope once said,
> "A bank is a place that will lend you money,
> If you can prove you don't need it."

One view of a credit card is the pre-approval for expedient loans. That is convenient, until the monthly bill comes in and you notice the double-digit interest charge. In many cases, up to three times or more than a bank would charge. So much for using pre-approved loans dressed up in plastic. We have conditioned ourselves to use 'borrowed' funds.

You would think that as people get older, these needs diminish. However, that is not necessarily the case. You are living off your liquid assets and social security when that urge arises. You know, the one that requires you to take that trip overseas or just to travel around the USA. You recognize the situation for what it is. You are going to take away dollars that help provide your monthly income.

Removal of capital from your savings will proportionately in most cases, reduce your monthly income. The reasons seniors take large withdrawals are not surprising. One frequent need is when your offspring ask for a loan to put down a deposit for a new home. You might have done this one yourself. It's usually a substantial loan and it's the loan that never gets paid back. Many children eventually look at it as a down payment on their inheritance.

If parents mention an unpaid loan made when these children visit them, they are going to see less and less of their grandchildren. Of course, the love remains, but asking for money back in many cases, creates its own road blocks, and things can get tense. When things grow tense, it makes family life needlessly, a little more difficult.

I heard this joke when some friends were talking about how money can affect relationships causing other bad scenarios. That's when one of them decided to share this,

> *"A couple who earlier had been discussing money matters were driving down a country road and they weren't speaking with one another. Their discussion had led to an argument and neither one wanted to concede their position. As they passed a farm with mules, goats and pigs, the husband asked sarcastically, 'Relatives of yours?' 'Yep,' his wife replied, 'in-laws."*

The straightforward program presented here can help take away the stress when unexpectedly having to finance large items, and in many instances, also reduce family tension. You will be even more amazed when you learn this concept is available even inside tax-qualified plans like a 401(k), and it doesn't have to take away from what you are currently doing. It can explode the value for every participant. Having it inside a 401(k) only adds to the value of the plan.

Recently I needed to purchase an item in a home improvement store. It is a well-known, national chain store found in almost every major city and town. I was behind another customer in the check-out line. As the cashier finished ringing up his order, the customer was told that he could save twenty percent on his purchase through the acquisition of a store credit card. The cashier used words that sounded at least to me, as if they were memorized.

Then came my turn to check out. I experienced the same storyline from this young cashier. The offer was given politely and it was made to sound lucrative. I asked what the interest rate might be. Without hesitation I heard, twenty-nine percent. My eyes opened up as I said, "Say what." The cashier seeing my expression as well, remarkably agreed with me and added that many customers have either previously acquired the card or take it when the purchase discount is offered. After calling it a crime, the cashier added that customers do use it when they come back for more supplies. The cashier went on to explain that some people use it because it doesn't impact on their credit cards.

There are a few people I know who literally brag at this point how much they save by using cash. I thought about that too, and then I did some math. When I hear this, I ask them how much return they are getting on their investments. I don't tell them, but I compound that figure mentally over five and ten years and I know the true cost of their purchase. Unfortunately, most people fail to recognize their loss of opportunity.

Isn't this fun? You lose money whether you finance or pay cash. While leasing isn't available on most purchases, if it were, mathematically it too would be a loser. What's a person to do?

When people are together and the discussion turns to money, you almost never hear talk about their credit cards, auto loans, home repairs and the total cost of their various purchases. No, they turn the discussion to investments and rates of return. They are all thinking what they could do with the extra money if only their investment returns improved. This kind of thinking is like boarding the wrong airplane at an airport. Looking back, many people wonder how they got on the wrong road.

"Do you have any good (investment) tips?" This question comes not from Advisor clients but others who know you are an Advisor. They are looking for something their own Advisor might not know or be sharing with them. They are looking for that magic wand to use on their money, looking for a shortcut to improve their financial position.

That question is one that those in my profession hear repeatedly. Whenever someone gives me a challenge like this, it makes me cringe. I'm thinking what they really mean is, "Is there something out there that can explode my rate of return."

When I give the answer, it comes out of left field for the other person. I try to do it politely and suddenly it's their turn, they cringe. They can't believe what I said. It gets more difficult, because the answer comes in just a few words, but the explanation can take up to a half an hour. Not because it's hard to understand, but because people have strong pre-conceived, yet incorrect beliefs on this subject, brought on by decades of misinformation.

While people in general know little about equities and bonds, some kick these around as if they were experts. They can't help themselves. They gain some information through television or the internet. Yet, what they are generally viewing is advertising to sell them on an idea, not knowledge.

The problem is that people think you have to be a good investor to make money, and that is just not true. In fact, everyone including good investors could do better if they learn how to enhance their investments.

True, you can make money by saving and investing, especially in qualified retirement plans like the 401(k). It's also a sad fact that the majority of Americans have almost all their savings inside retirement plans and Individual Retirement Plans (IRA).

HOWEVER, while participants think they are being smart putting almost all their savings into retirement plans, they are in fact hurting themselves and their families. They have lost access to their own money and given control over to the government.

Yes, there is another way, a proven better method to make substantially more money. To have access to your money, and enjoy a higher income than might be achieved otherwise.

You don't have to outperform in the market to acquire wealth, because you will have more money for investing and you will be able to do this without changing your lifestyle. One question that you may have is, if this is so good, why haven't I heard about this before. How about because even if it's been explained, there are decades of misinformation planted in their heads. Yet, this program has a long history, almost two centuries, of performing as advertised and it's not a secret.

Another answer might be that in our present culture, we don't give the traditional methods a chance. We want the latest, glitziest new methods. We want instant gratification and you know what else we've learned; the younger people today are smarter than us older folks. Just ask them or their teachers. They will tell you, they don't need to know how previous generations did things. History isn't important to them and then they fall into the old traps, the wrong traps.

We have lost contact over the past few years with a long-standing way of making money. We've become enthralled with the ads we see and hear. Feeling we're too smart and there's all these new ways of doing things, why then use old fashioned methods.

Maybe because some old-fashioned ideas work better than anything the bright young minds have developed. Funny thing, financial math doesn't change, just what we do with it.

You know who hasn't forgotten the old methods. It's the banks, many among the famous and the rich as well know this method, and they use it, big time. It serves the multi-millionaires in many ways. It can serve you as well.

We all want more money and we want it quick. If I am wrong, then the lottery system and casinos are making numbers up when it comes to the number of people who play to win, wanting to win with a now mentality.

I prefer to think that when we say most of us do want more money, what we are really saying is we want at least enough money to sleep well at night knowing that our needs, and maybe a few wants, are satisfied. We would like to be able to do those things we enjoy. Be free to buy the things we choose to buy, and have the time to enjoy them. We shouldn't be spending time thinking about financing our necessities.

According to statistics out of MarketWatch.com, the average young consumer will pay nearly $300,000 in interest over their lifetime. Does that grab your attention? It should, and it doesn't include inflation. In a typical family of five, that figure explodes to over a million dollars. That's your money, that's your family's money. It's throwing money away, you know, right into the bank's own accounts. It's no longer your money, it's theirs. You've raised your children to give away a million dollars, right?

However, unlike most taxes, interest is more controllable. In fact, why not consider keeping for yourself at least half of the interest payments you make every month. Neat, right? That's as good as getting a hefty pay raise at work, but that would be nice too.

Try thinking about it this way. For every bill you have to pay with interest, write two checks, one against the debt, and the other just for the interest. Add up all the interest for the month and multiply it by twelve. Surprise!

There are stumbling blocks that confront every one of us. Having goals and reaching them are two different things. Do we have to give up some of the things we want, so that we can have other things? It could be great if we can find a different way, a better way to go after the things we want.

Many advisors will suggest a tightening of the belt or giving up something you don't need. Of course, as you and I know, that's more easily said than done. There is a saying that, "A luxury once enjoyed, becomes a necessity." If you are like me, you don't want to give anything up.

I grew up in an era when if you wanted air conditioning in a car, you opened a window. It would be difficult to buy a new car today that didn't have air conditioning. We had to wind-up our Wristwatches and we were fortunate if they showed us the approximate time of day. They weren't like today's communicators (internet telephones) and GPS's. Now I too, find that I can't live without these new necessities.

Today, we live in an advanced society no matter how you measure it, and many of us don't want to be labeled as traditional. With new ideas daily and new terminology we look to the future and not to the past because that's the way of an evolving culture like ours. As I see it in this instance, tossing away traditional methods of doing things has blinded our younger generations. They have all the answers. After all, they are 'Progressive.'

In the end, we have to be responsible for ourselves. Society shouldn't have to save us although young people today are being given opinions to the contrary, especially in many institutions of higher learning.

You've heard this before but it must be repeated. If all the worlds' wealth was spread among the world's population, in ten years we would be back where we started. Ninety percent (that's 90%) of the wealth would once again be in the hands of the banks, insurance companies and Wall Street. As a society, we just refuse to learn from our mistakes, which in turn hurts all of us as individuals.

If we are going to succeed, we need a plan. It has to be workable and it has to be manageable, and of course, it has to be without much effort. After all, we are human beings and from my own experiences I believe being lazy is in our DNA. Therefore, the plan must not only be workable, it must be functional and easy for all those willing to commit to it, that is, to understand it and use it.

Having a plan is only part of the solution. You will need passion. People need passion for everything they do. Whether it's competitive sports, raising a family, or running a business, you will have trouble succeeding at the task at hand, without passion. You have to 'want' to free yourself from today's concepts on finance.

The great Yankee Clipper Joe DiMaggio came from a poor family and when asked where his drive for success came from, he said,

> *"A ball player has to be kept hungry to become a big leaguer. That's why no boy from a rich family has ever made the big leagues."*

While you can claim that statement isn't completely true today, it nonetheless goes to the heart of having the passion to succeed.

I once heard a very good professional baseball player ask, "What is the difference between an All-Star and a utility player? The question was theoretical and he went on to say, "A thin line between the ears." It takes both passion and confidence to succeed at anything you want.

Many people seek Advisors for the wrong reason. They want their Advisors to make them wealthy, but Advisors aren't magicians, although a few may make this claim.

It is my own belief that an Advisor is there to try and match your goals with your net assets. To help you make decisions about your money. To suggest the right portfolio for you keeping in mind your risk tolerance, your age and regularly monitor your path with suggestions for change when needed.

Brokers, Advisors, and many financial institutions advertise themselves as being best and they claim to bring the highest rates of return to their clients. They forget to mention what day of the month and in what month they accomplished that feat.

I love watching the television advertisements showing how the average person, utilizing a particular brokerage firm can retire, purchase an airplane, and fly it to the island they just bought. Surprising how many people fall into advertising traps. Yes, it's unfortunately true, it is a trap. In the minds of many people high returns reign supreme. It starts with the advertising and ending in collective minds.

Some Advisors and many investors use the Rate of Return as a measuring stick for achieving goals, although it is an artificial gauge. It supposedly tells them how well their money in the investment marketplace is doing over a specified period and it is frequently used, and at times, erroneously for comparisons. It doesn't tell them how well they are doing in their overall long-range planning. It is a measuring stick like a thermometer on the day, and only on the day you take its temperature.

I would like to share a somewhat familiar picture how an investment company could possibly advertise these numbers as their ROR and in turn, be misleading consumers whether deliberately or not. In this example, the investment company could claim, following a small down market that they made an average of 1.5% over 4 years, but how well did the investor do?

Amount Invested	$100,000	Earning Percentage
End of Year 1	$120,000	20%
Year 2	$117,600	-2%
Year 3	$135,240	15%
Year 4	$98,726	-27%

The investment company can make the claim for a positive average rate of return of 1.5%. However, the individual investor in the above example has a real loss of $1,274 over the four years with an Internal

Rate of Return of -0.32%. The investment company has a responsibility to show the methodology applied to those numbers.

Consider too, that reaching your financial goals becomes easier with more money invested as opposed to the idea that we can invest less and get higher returns. Advisors will tell you, or they should tell you that the more you save and invest, the more likely you are to achieve your long-term goals.

It is the amount you invest that will return you the volume you have at the end of the day. To say otherwise is to mislead. I too prefer a higher rate of return. That means more money in retirement. However, I believe people would prefer to have a higher cash flow to invest, while also enjoying a better lifestyle and enjoying it today.

"Great," thinking to yourself, "put away more money when I'm living off every dollar I make." That thought is so true for so many, regardless of the amount of income one has. I know a professional who earns nearly $360,000 after taxes and spends $380,000. Thankfully, for most of us including my friend the professional, given our own situations, this problem is solvable.

It's essential to keep in mind that having a strong investment portfolio isn't an answer for liquidity. It's usually designed for positive long-term results we may need for specific goals, but does nothing for you today, other than make you feel good.

There too, are those who are diligent savers and they are rightfully proud at what they have accomplished. However, there are many scenarios where money is needed and market timing can't be allowed to interfere with your needs. Using funds from an investment portfolio, especially during a down market equates to never seeing those dollars again, nor its potential earnings.

We have heard many clients say they were going to replace the dollars they took out of their accounts. They really believe it when they say it. The truth however, is that you can never replace the dollars you use. They are gone forever, both the dollars and the potential earnings.

Starting anew doesn't do it. Those are new dollars with new returns. The potential profits on the dollars taken from their accounts that were used for other purposes, are gone forever.

Buying a home, raising children, paying for other needs and wants, are good examples of where your money will go. When money is tight as it often can be, not only might the future look bleak, but the stress can and does build up, causing family turmoil.

I am a huge believer in Cause and Effect. It is an axiom describing everything we know and do. You may recognize this axiom as it is used extensively and wisely in seeking proof for God's existence. Additionally, in the final analysis, it goes to the result of everything we understand. That is, the Effect. This axiom can be seen frequently in the interaction between parents and children. Especially noticeable after something goes wrong in a home.

Whether scientists know it or not, and they probably do, they use this axiom for every theory they have or every experiment they carry out. To do otherwise is illogical.

To know where you are today, you have to recognize how you got here in the first place, the cause. "We are the sum of our experiences," said a professor in one of my economic classes just a few decades ago. Every now and then I reflect on that thought. It's so easy when looking back to realize that the dollars I used for other than my intended purposes are lost forever.

I went to a great high school where I never learned how to write a check, balance a home budget, or make financial decisions. My father was an Italian immigrant who barely spoke English explaining why we spoke Italian in the home. However, the nuns warned my parents at the end of my first year in school. They weren't letting me into second grade until I could speak English. That resulted into what I have come to call, one ugly summer. Yep, goes back to Cause and Effect. The consequences of which, I didn't know how to write a check even after graduating high school.

My parents were my life examples. I watched as my father worked overtime sweating it out as a laborer, praying he could find work on Saturdays just to help pay the bills. I would think to myself, "Are you crazy?" I didn't understand, it yet, but I had inherited his belief in duty and responsibility.

Today, I look back and appreciate the education I received. It was good. Yet, while we learned English, Math, Biology, etc., we didn't get the groundwork we needed to understand and how to use the dollar. We, and that's almost all of us to this day, pay the penalty for that failure. We can for instance, see this disaster unfold in the dollars we throw away when we borrow money from banks and other lenders.

A problem we have is that because we were never given the financial ground rules we need, we pay that penalty in an unrecognizable way. We are being held at gunpoint and we don't even know it. The government and the banks are holding the guns.

We save money, see something we want, then we buy it. If we don't have the necessary savings, we use our credit card. Then we start all over again. I once heard a foolish comment, yet so applicable to so many of us. I can't say for sure, but this had to have come from a credit card company.

"Anyone who lives within their means suffers from a lack of imagination."

We need to know how interest and taxes play a major impact on what we have left over for our style of living. Once you have a better understanding of the impact on your bottom line, you will want to utilize the method you will learn here. You can rearrange things in your favor, and at the end of the day enjoy having more dollars in your pocket.

Before you seek solutions, you have to have a better view of the problem. Once again, think of Cause and Effect. At some point we all cry foul. We wish we were in a better place financially giving us that independent freedom we seek. Regardless of where we are, we got here because of decisions and actions we took at some earlier date. The success we've had or the lack thereof, is a result of our own history, not the result of someone else putting us here.

The average American has this very large hole in their pocket for what was their money. By the way, this hole looks more like a "sink hole" than a hole on a golf course. Would you believe that approximately 30% of your income goes toward paying interest? That's right, once again, do the math, between Taxes and Interest, roughly 70% of your earned dollar is disappearing before your eyes. Hopefully, as we get into this, you will learn how to reduce these expenses.

<u>This is just as true for savers</u>. They don't realize it but they too are paying interest on their purchases. It's called 'lost' interest. They are writing the big checks at the time of making large purchases and are satisfied with their actions. *This is financially insane*.

Going into your retirement years, you may think you are paying less in taxes simply because your income has shrunk resulting in fewer dollars owed for federal and state income taxes. However, seniors pay taxes on the retirement funds drawn out of qualified accounts, and on the gain of other investments that are sold outside of IRA's.

We don't think of going to the bank and borrowing every time we make a purchase, but that is in essence what we are doing. Again, loans are created when we use credit. Nearly all large purchases use borrowed funds from a third party and there are big chunks of interest being lost every year. Lenders love this as witnessed by all the direct mail on refinancing mortgages or special credit card offers.

Americans move much more frequently today than we did a half century ago. We have fewer roots, families are scattered, jobs are on the move, children moving away and some of whom are later followed by parents to their new locations and their new homes mean new mortgages.

Reflecting on mortgages for a moment, I can't get over the number of people who believe advertisements and some Advisors who recommend doubling up on mortgage payments. Those extra dollars they argue, go toward the end of the mortgage saving you thousands of dollars.

What everyone seems blind to is the simple fact that if you are in a situation and have a financial emergency or where your income is suddenly gone, laid off at work, disabled or you quit, you will want liquidity. Since the bank isn't likely to lend you money-you aren't working-you can borrow money out of the 401(k) you have, and after that's gone, your family and friends will offer you the funds you need to go on living until you go back to work. Right? I'm sure they will come up with years of financial assistance if necessary. Just ask them.

The bank won't care about your situation, they want their payments. Those doubled-up payments you made well, without an escape plan, they may be worth less than a nickel about now, and you are on your own. Liquidity is king and you gave it away.

Going back to those advertisements about paying your home off in half the time and saving those future payments. It looked so good when you read it. When you think about it, you come to understand those are future payments inflation will have beaten down, and the loss of earnings on those dollars you might otherwise have had if you invested that additional money.

When people are young, they lament that they don't have money to save. Couples are too busy once they announce their engagement, and their wedding is going to cost a fortune. After they are married, they need a new home because once the wedding is history, they are getting ready for their first baby, and with the new home comes furniture, appliances, and maintenance. Later on, they are busy putting their three children through school.

Regrettably, in a scene I will keep banging away at, too many of us spend more time watching a single sporting event on television then we do the entire year planning our finances. Couples spend more time planning a vacation than discussing their finances in a year. What's wrong with that picture?

Nevertheless, finances must be an important subject, because most statistics have shown that more than fifty percent of all divorces are due to financial problems. Finances require discussion between a man and woman, and a willingness to plan together for both the short term and the long-term commitments as necessary.

Sadly, before you know it, people come face to face with their retirement, only to discover they should have started earlier, many years earlier, because now in their later years, their dollar has to do double duty. It has to help them with their daily living expenses and still pave the way ahead in preparation for retirement.

Of course, they saved when they could. They put a few dollars into the 401(k) at work with every paycheck and for those fortunate enough, their employers also contributed. When retirees discover that their retirement funds are insufficient it's too late to do anything about making a change.

Those closest to retirement are worried too, because they don't know if they'll have to find work or be able to manage off of what they have, and maybe losing the lifestyle they dreamed of having. Surprising few know how far their money in their retirement plan or IRA will not stretch. They have little idea as to how much their monies will provide for them over time. Not to mention, Retirees may have more expenses than they had when they were working.

Health expenditures and insurance premiums are a great example of what the unforeseen can hold, plus with all the free time, there's all those pleasurable things they've dreamed of doing that may now be in jeopardy.

There are the cars, vacations, roofs, homeowner association fees and many other items to add to their list of expenses. When you really weigh the future, many financial obstacles need to be addressed and planned for. I am not surprised that retirees still finance cars, homes and pull those credit cards out to make purchases knowing they will be repaying the cost and interest over time.

Not all that long ago, retirees had two primary goals. The first was to leave their family a legacy and the second goal, was not to worry about where they would spend their money. Those two goals are still in play, only now they read,
  1) Not to outlive their money and be a burden to their children
  2) They hope to have something left over as a legacy to their family.

The role reversal happened because we have a set amount of money saved at the start of our retirement, and thanks to medical advances in health care, we are living longer, a lot longer than our parents. Our money has to stretch further. Today, if we take two people living at age 65; we can expect at least one on average to reach age 92. Do not forget, taxes and interest never stop chewing on your dollar.

We recently had an elderly couple (ok, younger than me) in our office and reviewed their overall investment strategy. At the end of the conversation, I pointed out once more in the discussion, that they had nearly $800,000 in their IRA, and they should feel proud.

I then asked them, "What part of that $800,000 do you want your children to inherit in the event you both die tomorrow?" They responded as almost everyone else would, "We want them to get the full $800,000. We worked hard for that money and it's going to them."

No argument! They put that money away and did it at times with some hardship. In my mind, they deserve it. However, in real life it does not work that way. I showed them the two options available to their children. One method popularly called a 'stretch' IRA allows that the children can stretch out the income from the IRA for their anticipated lifespan. Taxes are paid on the income they are required to take from the IRA. Funny thing about that, after understanding their options, young people almost always want it in cash, and that's what they elect to do, take it in cash.

I used a white board we have in our conference room. I put $800,000 at the top and then drew an arrow pointing down from that number. At the bottom of the arrow, I wrote the number $500,000 and explained that the government was in the line ahead of their children to take money from the IRA. Not exactly a small amount either. The children would be paying both income and inheritance taxes on the sum they inherited. The dollars their parents worked so hard to save.

They were shocked. They really had no idea that a number as high as that shown could be confiscated by the government. Of course, there were solutions to their situation, but this pointed out problems with most forms of money, even the money many believe they have protected from attack.

You should keep in mind at all times that your money is under attack daily. Sadly, the government is first in line and it wants every penny it can get. Every time you finance something, somebody wants another piece of your pie.

Again, getting older doesn't stop you from wanting many of those things you desired when you were younger. That money you saved might just be burning a hole in your pocket unless you make the effort to protect it. There are many more mistakes made by the "experienced" generation than you would imagine.

One picture of us getting older has us being forced to withdraw money from our retirement plans-required minimum distributions-and paying taxes on those funds. If we need supplemental income or a large withdrawal to help a family member, we are going to pay taxes on those dollars.

Overall, it's frightening each time we think of the overall impact on our lifestyle that comes from the massive "Volume" of taxes and interest. Imagine what you could do if you didn't have or could reduce those two major obstacles to your bottom line.

How many times have we all heard someone say, "I just wish I had a few extra dollars," or "I keep hoping I will get a raise soon, I've earned it, and besides, I really could use that money now?"

Problem with these and similar statements comes with the realization that those dollars too, would disappear one way or another. It should not come as a surprise, but you know, the more money many people earn, the more they spend. The more things they buy, the more they will need financing.

It's a revolving door and we don't seem able to help ourselves. Nearly every month there is an article claiming that personal debt has increased again. This holds just as true in an abundant economy as it is during a recession.

Chapter 2

The Endangered Dollar

> **"When Money realizes that it is in good hands,
> it wants to stay and multiply in those hands."**
> Idowu Koyenikan

Nothing is as devastating to one's lifestyle then taxes and interest. As we examine taxes and interest, we will drill into a couple of methods to avoid paying as much as we do in taxes that is possible and cut into interest in a big way. Reducing these expenses by any amount is worth the effort.

The interest we pay on financing purchases is controllable. In fact, it may be possible as you will discover, that interest payments don't have to be made unless you want to pay them. You read that right. It is at your discretion whether to make the interest payments or not. As we unlock what I consider the best option available for financing anything you buy on time, I think nearly all who read these pages will in the end, make informed decisions which will benefit them.

TAXES

There are four places your money goes, no matter who you are. These four include taxes, interest on financed purchases, lifestyle dollars and savings. I know the first time I saw this chart, it was difficult for me to believe. I mean, I majored in Economics and Finance. Shouldn't I have known this information all along? Shouldn't you have known?

This pie chart illustrates where the average earned dollar goes, that is the money you earn while at your place of employment. Some may wish to dispute this, but I believe this information will be in step with your situation and nearly all others as well. It really doesn't matter what your socio-economic position is, the information here is applicable to most of us who have to earn a living, and even those few, who don't have to work.

There goes the money!

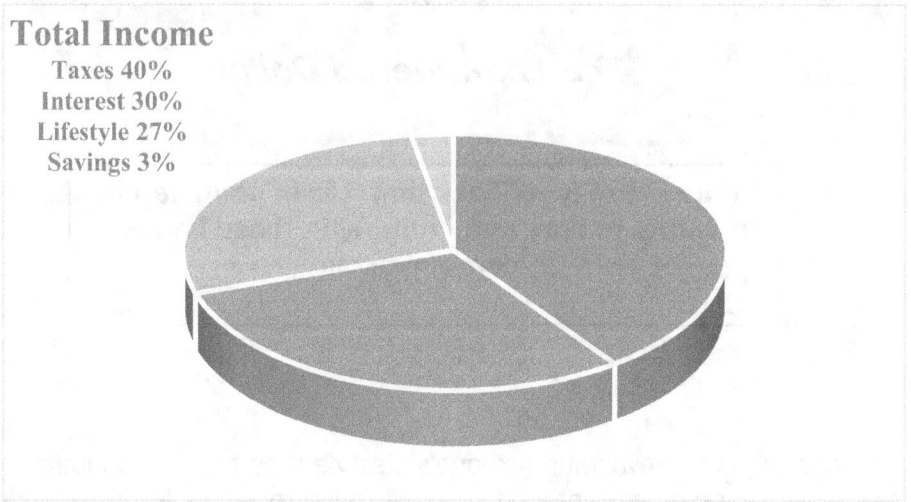

Total Income
Taxes 40%
Interest 30%
Lifestyle 27%
Savings 3%

What's going on? How is this possible? You may never think about it, but the government has more of your paycheck to spend than you do. Why does the government get to spend more of my paycheck than I do? How did that interest sneak up on me and now that I know this, how do I get out of this trap and keep more for myself?

Imagine! Every dollar earned on average yields approximately 40 cents to the government. That doesn't seem possible because you are thinking, "I'm in a 15% overall income tax bracket." However, when you take a moment and focus your attention, you come to a different conclusion. You may earn $75,000 each year and say, "But the government only gets $11,250." Is that so? Is that what you really believe? Because if you do, you had better think again. You only see direct taxes in your paycheck, it's all those other sneaky ones they nail you with.

We have all sorts of taxes to pay, and while we may only occasionally notice these numbers on a receipt or in some other way, we do know we are paying added taxes. We just never take the time to add them up, maybe we are afraid of what we will see.

Deception and sleight of hand tactics are being used so much, they are easily discernable and now look almost archaic. Yet, those in control continue to use these 'hidden' taxes to keep our citizens at bay.

However, we need not visit that argument. Rather we need to know where we are.

Some taxes are very visible; others are not:

Federal Income Taxes	State Income Taxes
Social Security Taxes	Medicare Taxes
Real Estate Taxes	Municipal Income Taxes
State Sales Taxes	Entertainment Taxes
Insurance Premium Taxes	Highway Toll Taxes
Gasoline Taxes	Automobile Purchases
Dining Out Taxes	the List goes on

It's fair to say, taxes are wealth killers. An accountant was overheard saying,

"One difference between death and taxes,
is that death doesn't get worse every time Congress meets."

We have become so used to sales taxes that we never get shocked when making any kind of purchase. I will however admit, that seeing a tax for $3,000 added onto a $50,000 car is a shocker. You negotiate the car's price, agree to the purchase and then there it is, on the sales slip, "sales tax," and with the amount. Like you, I look twice and realize there is seemingly no getting around this. It adds a little curl to your stomach, but doesn't stop you from signing. I think to myself, "Smart car salesman, waited until I was committed and then mentions it as he goes over the sales agreement."

Heck, a married couple probably spends a thousand dollars a year on gasoline taxes alone. In my home state, as of now, we have the largest gasoline tax in the country and pay a total of $.77 on every gallon. I'm so fortunate to live in Pennsylvania. Just think, $.77 on every gallon and my state gets $.59 of it. That's a fixed cost and there is discussion to increase it. You do the math.

We may never even notice that most states are in some stage of increasing the tax on gasoline because the politicians know they will only hear from a few of us and the rest will miss this spot on the nightly news.

They can and do, always blame the price for a gallon of gasoline on the oil companies, at least the politicians do. Makes them look like angels as they falsely tell us how they are fighting the large oil companies. They know too that in no time at all, we will forget about it.

The number one expense in our lifetime is taxes. Not your home, not your cars, it's taxes. We tend to forget that the volume of taxes we pay doesn't stop at the paycheck. The government takes more overall, then you have left to spend on your lifestyle.

Call it what you want: Income Tax, Sales Tax, Real Estate Tax and more. It still adds up to 40 cents on the dollar, your dollar.

Think about it,

- ✓ **You earn it – they tax it** (income taxes)
- ✓ **You spend it – they tax it** (sales taxes)
- ✓ **You invest it – they tax it** (income taxes and/or capital gains taxes,)
- ✓ **You live in it – they tax it** (real estate taxes on your home)
- ✓ **You die – they tax it** (state inheritance taxes, federal estate taxes)

It's as if politicians think that if you can't see it, they can take it, and it won't hurt their re-election efforts. As a former IRS Director famously said,

> *"There is a difference between a tax collector and a taxidermist –*
> *the taxidermist leaves the hide."*

One of my favorite potential taxes is that on General Obligation Municipal Bonds. I call this a 'sneaky' hidden tax. No, not for the owners of those bonds, but for the local taxpayers in the municipality issuing those bonds. When you go to the polls and approve a bond, you are approving a loan against yourself guaranteeing that your taxing authority will pay both the interest and the principal. It is amazing how many voters are out in left field on this one.

If the governing authority fails to be able to make the required timely payments for lack of funds, it then has the power to tax the people in its district to make the loan whole, and you can't yell foul. You see, you authorized the tax when you voted for the bond. There is a reason they call these General Obligation Municipal Bonds.

Any doubt how the average middle-class American can pay 40% of their income in tribute to the government......I hope not!

Well, maybe you think that's not too bad. You say to yourself that I still have 60 cents left over and that puts me in the same boat as everyone else. Yes, it very well may put you in that same boat, but we aren't done because you shouldn't like the boat, and you should want to get out.

While the government uses every means possible to collect as much as possible from your paycheck, but you have a right to strategize tactics that result in less taxation. In fact, I agree with those who believe you have an obligation to do so.

> **"Anyone may arrange his affairs so that his taxes shall be as low as possible; he is not bound to choose the pattern which best pays the treasury. There is not even a patriotic duty to increase one's taxes. Over and over again, the Courts have said that there is nothing sinister in so arranging affairs as to keep taxes as low as possible. Everyone does it, rich and poor alike and all do right, for nobody owes any public duty to pay more than the law demands."**
> **Judge Learned Hand, Judge, U.S. Court of Appeals**

And yet, we do pay more than the law demands. Perhaps some of us mistakenly think of paying our taxes as an act of Patriotism. Perhaps we are lazy and would just rather pay our taxes without drilling down to see what can be avoided, or getting help from professionals, especially accountants. Please remember that there is a legal difference between avoiding and evading. Trying to evade taxes puts you into another, completely different category. A place you don't want to be in.

Going back a few years, we had a client come in who was interested in adding to his bond portfolio. He had two goals in mind, safety, and tax avoidance. He loathed the idea of paying taxes and did not want anything that would require paying taxes.

This didn't give us much in the way of options. Although for this gentleman, there were some 'alternative' tax-free investments, these alternatives did not fit into his risk tolerance. However, they did work with his desires not to pay a penny to the government unless absolutely required. He would refuse any strategy that wasn't both safe and tax-free.

When we finished reviewing his options, he chooses quality tax-free municipal bonds and nothing else. Now, other bonds at that time had higher yields, municipals were around 3.5%. He went with the municipal bonds because the earnings were federally income tax free. It was explained to him that he could take the higher yielding bonds, pay taxes in his bracket and net a higher return. Financially it made sense, but he was adamant about not paying taxes, he went with the municipal bonds. Go figure!

As I have said, I am against paying taxes, but not so much against taxes as to be foolish about it. The government has given us tax "loop-holes." Not just for the rich as advertised by some politicians, but for all of us. It's just that those who know how to use the laws to their advantage get 'richer.'

The government makes tax laws and then conveniently makes exclusions for them. If for instance, you follow the rules of the road, you can put money into a tax-qualified retirement plan such as a company 401(k) Plan or an IRA, called tax 'qualified plans.' They created these 'exceptions' to help us prepare for retirement, which they can do, but beware the dangers from the traps politicians set for us.

The government actually likes tax-qualified retirement plans. You wouldn't think that because they are tax deductible for contributions made to the plans out of individual earnings. That's less money coming in for them to spend.

However, the government loves tax-deductible programs because you and your family will end up paying even more in taxes. Maybe, at the time they created these qualified plans their intentions were good, but we should think twice about that.

If you decide to remove funds from your 401(k) plan, there are taxes due on those monies and, if you do take funds prior to age 59 ½, there is a 10% penalty as well. For the Traditional plans, should you fail to take required distributions past age 70 ½, there is a more serious penalty for your failure to do so.

Let's say you are past 70 ½ years of age and fail to take the required minimum distribution from your qualified IRA account. We'll assume you were to withdraw $10,000 but instead you left it in the account. You think to yourself that you are in a 20% income tax bracket, so the IRS will tax you for $2,000 as they would have done had you taken the withdrawal on time. Well, you're wrong, the IRS wants 50% of what you failed to withdraw. That's called a fine. Yes, the IRS wants $5,000, that's 50%.

Let's not forget that $2,000 for income taxes. The total cost comes to $7,000. For those of us old enough to remember, there was a picture of Uncle Sam pointing toward you and saying, "Uncle Sam Wants You." That was a worthwhile attempt to pull in recruits to serve our country. Well, now they could use that same picture and change the wording to, "Uncle Sam Wants Your Money."

Once more going back to Cause and Effect, the IRS needs your taxes to keep the government running, but running the government isn't the problem. It's holding back all those politicians who use your money to be re-elected. They have a tight stranglehold on the nation and they want to maintain their power. To keep you voting for them, they feel the need to give your money away especially to projects or groups where the voters, after the politicians justify their actions, reward the politician with votes.

As you very much aware in today's world of quick news, politicians look at their best when the giving is in the form of entitlements, grants and just about anything, that catches the voters' attention in a positive way. We never really know the motives, but at the end of the day, the Cause is political power. The Effect of all their good deeds is the fuel we lovingly call taxes.

I know everyone reading this remembers when a man running for President made the claim, "I don't pay taxes," everyone and not so quietly, rebelled. Almost everyone was appalled at the thought that a man who could become President of the United States didn't pay taxes.

Instead they should have wanted to learn how he did it, and could they replicate what he did. Politicians screamed aloud about his being non-patriotic, but who were they kidding. They too, avail themselves of similar opportunities at every chance they get.

From all available information, he used one of the best tax shelters in our nation, real estate. He made sure he followed the rules. Instead of people complaining, they should be asking for the name of his accountant.

For our purposes here, real estate doesn't work. I'll state that again. It doesn't work for our intended purpose. It is an illiquid investment and carries too much risk. Yet, ironically, and as will be shown, real estate returns can be increased significantly when applying the method in this book.

Many millionaires got where they are, because they knew how to beat the 'system.' In our solution to building your own wealth, taxes and interest play a part. Depending on your own situation, the part it plays is up to you. Either way, you will learn how to keep more of your money, much more money providing security for you and your family.

Remember what Judge Learned Hand had to say.

"Anyone may arrange his affairs so that his taxes shall be as low as possible,
he is not bound to choose the pattern which best pays the Treasury."

INTEREST

A young couple, John and Betty together earn $90,000 per year, from all outward appearances they are successful. They recently purchased a home, need two cars and they like most people, use credit cards. During one review, they shared the following information,

They Have	Monthly Payment	Interest	Annual
Home	$ 2,210	$ 1,742	$ 20,904
2 Cars	$ 755	$ 191	$ 2,292
Credit Cards	Interest only	$ 188	$ 2,256
Store credit	$ 45	$ 27	$ 324
Credit Union	$ 180	$ 54	$ 648
Total Interest		$ 2,202	$ 26,424

That's a nice chunk of interest going out every month, after tax no less. Putting this number down and computing the total, the volume of interest being paid over the next five years with everything remaining the same, comes to an unbelievable $132,120. Even if you discount future payments reducing the mortgage interest, this is a remarkable amount of money being thrown to the wolves. Not that bankers and other lenders are wolves, it's just that they make their money by taking it from the rest of us.

The interest in the example above represents 29.3% of John and Betty's gross income. The numbers do not reflect other financed items with interest due for other purchases such as those from department stores where the interest typically runs beyond 20%. This couple may have also financed a computer on line or bought a new refrigerator. Interest just keeps building up. That's washing away what could be a healthier lifestyle. Just the cars and credit cards as shown above account for 5% of their income, a very bothersome amount by themselves.

WOW! Between taxation and interest on purchases and a mortgage, the total amount disappearing from paychecks can easily exceed 70%. That is excessive. We can blame part of this on government confiscation. The other part is our own fault. Yes again, that's our money going down the proverbial 'hole' in the ground.

For the average working family, they are left with potentially less than 30% to spend on their lifestyle, and out of that of course, comes their retirement savings, money for emergency needs as well as for opportunities. They are living on just a net 30% of their income. It really is a bleak picture.

Can't say this enough, next time you look at your paycheck, just think about where that after-tax amount is going. The odds are it isn't going where you would like it to go. Odd that we ignore this, but I understand, life has stuff going on and we can't be bothered.

I want you to envision sitting at your kitchen table and looking at $20,000 on a placemat in front of you. The majority of those utilizing the method you learn in this book can at the least, save that $20,000 you are visualizing, every five years, while most will save even more. There really is no ceiling to this.

This method doesn't take away from anything you are doing. You won't be sacrificing anything. In fact, the design should enhance your ability to purchase the items you may want to acquire. All you need is a passion to succeed and a discipline you can live with every day. The discipline too, is a simple procedure, which doesn't take anything away from you.

Every day we are assaulted with seductive offers. These offers which in effect, give our money away to banks and lenders continue to find their way into our mailboxes. Oh, those advertisements don't say they want us to give them our money and put it in their pockets, but that's what they are doing.

The offers come in from money lenders informing us that they have (or what may appear to be) low interest rates, enticing us to borrow large sums of cash. Mortgage companies wanting to refinance our homes at a lower rate. Banks offering cash to start an account with them. Other lenders offering us cash for any reason. The offers help us to fantasize about how we would use that money while they are suggesting they have lower rates than their competitors. It must work for the lenders because they keep advertising.

I love the headlines, "Get out of debt faster while paying less." This was from a recent offering for a zero percent introductory offer to switch to another credit card. From the firing pan into the fire. It's like offering someone a free taste of fudge on the Atlantic City Boardwalk. They seduce us with those samples and we go in to satisfy our new hunger. We know what can happen after that.

The Credit Card Companies in particular are in hot pursuit and who can beat their special offers if you sign by next week. These companies do it through the mail, radio, and television, and of course, on the internet. It's tough to resist unless you read the twenty or more lines in 'tiny' print. You would be amazed at the warnings. That zero percent interest for the first six months will melt away when you see the eleven percent or more after the initial period. I've seen offers that go from the introductory offer to as high as twenty-nine percent depending on credit scores.

It gets even better. You don't want to miss the part in that fine print where you pay twenty percent or more if you are late on a payment.

"Because you have 'good credit' the letter started, the bank has a personal line of credit available to you. Collateral not needed, get up to $100,000 at 9%. It gets you thinking about all the things you would like to do or to have if you had that money. They've made it so easy, so tempting. Such a deal!

Until today, you have had limited options when making large purchases. You can finance an item by using your credit card or making a loan. The other option preferred by a few, is to pay for it out of savings. Both methods are wrong. You are giving your money, your wealth to someone else.

You've seen these advertisements in the mail and through other media,

"Get rid of credit card debt,
Transfer your account to our card
And pay no interest for 2 years."

I prefer this advertisement,

"Get rid of credit card debt,
Transfer your account to us
Pay on your terms, not ours
And NEVER have to pay interest again."

No need to worry, we have a rescue plan that will stun you since you would never before have thought so, from what you hear so often.

When you use credit, the interest you pay may seem small on each cyclical invoice. Yet, if you take the time to add up all your monthly interest payments over the course a month, multiply that number by twelve, you can see the mountainous volume of interest you are throwing down the drain, never to be seen again.

Using your own money is no better. I will say this over and over again, when you calculate the cost of money, the potential loss on capital is huge, and it has a multiplier effect. This is a compounding interest charge 'loss.'

As was mentioned earlier, 30% of our money going to interest is an amazing percentage of our paychecks. Not only do you get to pay the government more than you net for lifestyle, you also pay interest in an amount by itself that often is greater than the cash that is left over for 'lifestyle' spending and saving. This has to go. If we can reduce taxes by any amount and then cut a considerable chunk out of the interest we pay, lives will change, and they will change for the better.

A few years ago, a man and a woman came in for a review of their investment accounts. This married couple had over $600,000 in their IRA accounts. That was their "liquid" accounts. They certainly weren't broke, but they couldn't easily use their 'qualified' funds without paying taxes and losing the potential of that money forever.

They had just enough in their regular savings and checking accounts in their credit union to get them through the next four weeks if necessary. It was their way of addressing their 'emergency' needs.

Among the items discussed that day was a charge from a well-known computer marketing company. They were getting late monthly notices because they had fallen behind with that particular bill. There were too many distractions in their life and paying bills had to wait. They had the money; they didn't have the time to make payments. Why pay it today when you can pay it tomorrow?

I looked at their bill and noticed they had purchased $3,000 of computer equipment. From their invoice and what I learned from them, they had already paid $3,000 over three years and somehow owed another $3,400, and that number could go up. Their payments were for the most part going to interest. At the time of purchase, they heard the salesperson on the telephone say "interest free for 12 months." Their hearing probably shut off at that point.

I considered the possibility to myself that they probably thought they were getting a deal when they made that purchase, and maybe they were. Yet, they were paying more than double the amount they financed. Yeah, they thought they had a great deal!

They acted surprised when I showed them the numbers, but I suspect they were aware of the numbers before they came in that day. They had initially intended to pay off their purchase within the time frame allowing for zero percent. When they failed to do that, the debt exploded.

They came in that day hoping I might have an idea that could help them. I reminded them that I'm an Advisor, not a wizard. Nonetheless, before they left that day, they were given a not-perfect, but usable solution based on their circumstances. Their purchase was paid off in full the following week.

A young couple walks into a 'home care' type department store and the first thing they see is that new tractor lawn mower that's just perfect for their needs. They ask the clerk working that area how much the mower costs. He says, "It's just $9,293. It's a steal at that price, it's normally $10,325," he explains that you are getting more than a thousand dollars off the regular price, quite a deal.

The salesman continues and explains that they can get another 10% off by applying for the 'store' credit card. Still, it's a lot of money, but they totally want this mower. The husband turns toward his young wife and says with a smile, "You know, we can do this." She loves him and she knows this is something he has wanted for some time, so she says without giving it too much thought, because of her love for him, "Ok," adding her own little smile.

Because they plan to pay the credit card bill off in 3 years, their interest, and the taxes on the mower alone would total $4,178 bringing the total cost of the mower to $12,933. Remember, it's a steal at that price. Question, who's doing the stealing?

Isn't it strange that after we negotiate a purchase for something we want, and at what appears to be a good price, we charge it and always fail to include interest into the cost of that purchase? Somehow, as we look at the bill presented to us at time of purchase, we see the interest as just an add-on at the check-out counter, something not to worry ourselves with.

Your next-door neighbors are excited as they share the news with you that they are about to make an addition to their home. The addition will cost approximately $45,000, so they are going to the bank to borrow the money because that's what everybody does. Financially they seem okay. They have nearly $540,000 in their retirement plans where they work, but using that money is really out of the question because they learned it introduces risk of opportunity lost in an up market, then there are all the restrictions as well. Not to mention, the loan would have to be paid off in five, not ten years.

They have personal debt including paying off long term educational loans and credit cards. They keep about $3,000 or slightly more in the bank for emergencies. Their mortgage balance is nearly 70% of their home value and they have been late a few times making the payments thanks to their lackadaisical behavior.

The bank manager explains he can give them the funds they need, but because of their overall financial position and credit score, the interest rate will be 11%. That's when they think to themselves, "It could be worse," as they justified how the addition would pay for itself when they sold their home. They were also aware that they couldn't collateralize their qualified plan monies and agreed to take the bank's offer. Banks cannot collateralize qualified retirement accounts because these funds are sheltered and creditor-proof inside a "trust," the plan. The bank would not have access.

They took the loan for ten years with monthly payments of $657. Their total payments for the $45,000 would amount to $78,848, which includes total interest of $33,848. That's an average interest payment of $282 every month for the next ten years. Yikes!

The interest payments have zero value and represents a serious hit. That's money they'll never see again. "What the heck," and like most people they thought, its spread out over ten years. There were a few other fees as well, but nothing significant. What a Wonderful World!

Let's look at the options,

	Monthly	Total Payments	Over
The Lender's Way	$ 657	$ 78,848	120 months
Option 1	$ 477	$ 57,275	120 months
Option 2	$ 652	$ 53,175	81 months

'Option 1' reflects making payments over the same period of time, but at a significantly lower amount each month. We do this by eating away at the interest rate for the loan. Doing it our way saves $21,573. Nice pocket change!

Following the path in 'Option 2' above, the payments saved are $25,623. That's $25,623 out of pocket. Same product, same payment as for the Lender, only difference is the 39 less monthly payments.

That's not the end of the story. Doing it the bank's way, the money is gone. Nothing else to show for it except for the additional cost.

Under both Options 1 and 2 above, they would have money in their 'savings' account. The totals depending on contract and time, would be between $60,000 and $80,000. That's their money, in their own savings account. It doesn't belong to the lender.

Imagine that! The neighbors can save more than $21,000 in payments and all they have to show for it, other than the finished product, is another $60,000 or more in their savings account.

I don't know about you, but to me and most others, this is a huge difference, and the choice is yours to make.

The traps are everywhere, even for people who save money for a 'rainy' day. I remember a situation where an elderly woman had nearly $30,000 in a conservative mutual bond fund. That was money she had set aside for emergencies. For years, she had faithfully put $100 every month into her account and felt comfortable with the type of bonds the fund purchased.

One day her 45-year-old daughter came to her. The daughter was in trouble. She was behind in her bills and even worse for her, the mortgage was months behind. She was going to get everything caught up, but she said it would take time. She needed a little help from her mother. In fact, she needed $10,000, and she claimed she needed it quick.

This was her daughter and mom didn't think twice about it. Without looking at different options, she checked her mutual fund and it was now at $26,000 following a 'market' adjustment, but it was more than sufficient to help her daughter. She had the mutual fund company send her a check for $10,000 and she handed the money over to her daughter.

Now, that fund was down to $16,000. The daughter if she was like most, would not likely pay mom back anytime soon. With little to no chance for the fund to make up the loss and the disbursement, there wasn't much hope that the funds given to her daughter and with the current state of the market would ever be made whole. The shares sold at low prices cannot be replaced.

This scene happens too often. Parents don't realize there are other methods to help their children. Methods where they won't lose their money and the children get what they said they needed.

Have you ever wondered why you put money into a bank that gives you 2% (taxable) on your dollars, but then lends that same money back to you at 8%? Not only that, they then lend the same money out again, maybe to a small business and get 12%. All of this from your deposit.

Of course, they explain how a bank has a lot of overhead. Their technology is costly. They have employees and then there are those branches and the associated cost to running a bank. They also have another expense. Do not ignore it. It's too big! You see, they have stockholders who expect something back for their investment.

With all this overhead, it's no wonder they charge you more than you get on your savings. Besides they argue, how else would they be able to pay that 2%? I once heard,

Bankers are people that help you with problems,
You would not have had without them.

Chapter 3

The Magic

> **"A life is not important except in the impact it has on other lives"**
> **Jackie Robinson**

I had no idea that I would be doing this, sharing financing intelligence with everyone, but life happens. I knew what I had to say is important and like Jackie Robinson, I wanted it to make an impact on people's lives.

The following narrative is a most effective summary for those that read this book. It is not new, but the analogy of what you are about to learn is powerful.

There were three Arabian horsemen riding through the desert late in the day. As the horsemen were looking for a place to put their tent for the night when they came across an Angel. After a greeting, the Angel instructed them to put sand in their pockets. Waking in the morning they would be both happy and sad.

The next morning upon waking, the three horsemen reached into their pockets. They were startled to see the sand they put in the night before had turned into diamonds. They were deliriously happy. Then, after a moment, they were sad. They were sad that they had not put more sand in their pockets.

At the time this book began, I was looking for a way to share my story, one that I learned fifty years ago with the Connecticut Mutual.

My first day in this business, April Fool's Day in 1969, I was handed sales material to help me sell their products. I hated that we were made to memorize four pages of a presentation, but I came to learn it was a great story, effective and on target.

It took me a week to memorize and adapt to it. When my supervisor heard me give the presentation, he approved. He was turning me loose. I could fly solo. Then he said to me, "Now you have to put the material in your own words. It has to come from you." I did. It was rewarding to see how quickly my audience grasped the idea, because the presentation did cover all the bullet points people needed to know. I used this material for decades with many people, and hundreds became clients.

One day this past year while surfing on YouTube, I spotted what appeared to be a very interesting title. I decided to check it out and watched a four-minute performance

The Advisor doing the presentation, Kyle Davis in Florida brings a refreshing breathe of air to an old story. He does it in a great, animated manner, one that there is no way I could replicate. After viewing a few short clips, he had put on YouTube, I called him and congratulated him on his great productions.

Kyle was rapidly becoming an inspiration for me. Speaking with Kyle, I couldn't help but notice that he remained throughout our conversation, the same dynamic individual I had watched on YouTube.

Initially, after viewing the videos and while speaking with Kyle, I had an unsettled feeling as I began thinking, "Where have I been for the past 5 decades?" He did it in such a nice easy way, entertaining and well animated. I knew there were changes to make in my presentation and a desire to drill down deeper into the material. I couldn't wait to get started. I had to get my own story out.

Today with nine grown children, I realized I wanted to share my story with them. However, like many children in recent years, they never listen to dad. If knowledge were coming from me to them, it wouldn't get a second look. Something different had to be done. At my advanced age, there was a sense of urgency.

I decided to write a short booklet so they along with friends and clients could see a new perspective on what I had been saying for years. This story is that important to me. As I started doing this, the idea hit me that I should share this not only as I originally intended, but with everyone else. If I really believe in this, then it is too important and powerful not to spread the news.

It is my desire to open up to everyone I can reach, to help each person have an opportunity to improve their lifestyle and happiness, **to help each one, enjoy their family and to free them from many of their financial worries**.

When you see the program initially, all of your previous misconceptions are going to cross your mind, and you will pull back. Having seen this initial effect on others, I can only anticipate your immediate reaction.

Therefore, I think it might be a good idea before that introduction to mention a few people for support, people who have successfully used this program. It's not some hidden secret, some of those who used it are well known, and there are many available sources supporting this.

In the order they will appear later;

Walt Disney
J.C. Penney
Ray Kroc
U.S. Senator John McCain

While their stories are verifiable there are stories on others that I found interesting as well. That would include the Vanderbilt and the Rothschild families. Yet, the greatest success stories come from Middle America, the average American, not the super wealthy.

No, you don't need to be wealthy. You need to understand this concept, have a desire to control your expenditures on your larger purchases, and the passion to follow through for success.

Let's start with a simple axiom. "Everything you purchase is financed." It doesn't matter if you charge it with credit, or you use cash. As you will see,

"You bought it, You financed it."

According to Nasdaq.com, consumer debt in America is rising at an alarming rate. The average household has thousands in credit card debt alone, followed by thousands in student loan debt and many thousands more in various loans. These are worrisome problems.

In the Introduction, I referred to an intriguing N.Y. Post article published on April 2, 2018. Desiring to validate the information, I searched many internet sites and found the statistics contained in the article to be consistent with other sources.

The article pointed out that the medium family balance on credit cards to be $15,983, and the average annual interest charge to be 18.6%. Therefore, it wasn't a shock to read that new credit card accounts have an average APR (Annual Percentage Rate) of 16.73% according to Creditcards.com.

Doing research on this, I found that people don't realize they are using Credit Cards to borrow money. Not too advanced a reality, but one we frequently overlook. Every time we use our credit cards, there is a corresponding loan.

Still, another article provided data pointed to another statistic, one that was more difficult to grasp. Simply, that 43% of credit card holders pay the interest only on their cards. Nothing like rolling the debt over without having anything to show for it.

Nasdaq.com has a multitude of interesting data, much of which applies to you and me. Here are a few debt statistics found there from 2018,

> The median student loan debt is for a student who attended and/or graduated college is in excess of $49,000.
> The household median credit card balance is now more than $16,000.
> The average auto loan is in excess of $30,000.
> Personal loans and miscellaneous debts are more than $10,000 per household.

Some may argue that not all families have student loans outstanding, and those numbers aren't applicable to them. I'll agree with that noting there are types of loans not included here. However, the remaining $56,000 debt in that number is more common than most folks might think, and it's true in tens of millions of homes.

Credit cards and personal loans are among the top resources for making desired purchases and in some cases, making ends meet. It is unnerving to see people reach for their credit cards for small purchases rather than use cash. To use credit cards to purchase food in a store is to me, incredibly foolish. We both know that there are times when we don't pay our entire credit card bill and that means that there is an interest charge on the food we ate last month.

Every time the Fed raises interest rates, credit cards get more expensive, and quickly. The cards have become acceptable continuous revolving debts and somebody is making quite a bit of money off of everyone else. One last surprise for me was from a Poll showing that over half of credit card users are clueless about their annual percentage rate (APR). In addition, they don't know whether it includes fees and other expenses, sometimes not reflected in the APR.

I did the math and quickly determined that the average debt holder was throwing $5,600 in interest per year into someone else's retirement plan. If one's after-tax take home pay is $50,000, this is the equivalent to giving away 11.2% of their spendable paycheck annually. That's $5,600 that this person will never benefit from or see again. For many people this is a nonstop give away, the proverbial revolving door of debt.

I arbitrarily used a charge of 10% on the debt, because it should not even be arguable especially after seeing many interest rates intolerably higher, on different client statements.

In this example, if we only paid the interest of $466 for seven years on this total debt, we would still owe $56,000 at the end. You have to ask yourself, 'Why do people do this?'

You have to want to put away money for future emergencies and you have two banks to choose from. There is the standard bank down the street and then there is the alternate one.

· This alternate bank offers many features for saving money. It puts the money in a vault after charging you a small buy-in cost. It quickly allows the needed financial flexibility through its provisions when needed. You can begin using the savings in advantageous ways you never before imagined.

That cash savings will be credited with more interest than the lender is charging you. This is the only liquid asset, providing so many guaranteed interrelated uses with positive leverage available. While the interest earnings may be slightly higher for the first ten years in a typical bank, this alternate bank begins paying the higher rate of interest going forward.

The money in this alternate bank is growing free of taxes. It's non-reportable to the government and its creditor-proof in most states.

The money in this alternate bank can provide strong, supplemental retirement income, tax-free income (following the proper procedures).

When using your account for financing or any other purpose you, not someone else, sets the amount and period to pay any loans used. You could pay interest only and through the use of 'bank' dividends retire the debt. You set the method, the amount, and the period.

No one sends you notices if you fail to pay one month, two months, fourteen months, etc. Your credit score is not impacted. As a matter of fact, since this loan isn't shown anywhere, it's private, your credit score should be stronger.

Once you and your agent properly structure a suitable payback, you can pay off any debts with a loan from our Guaranteed Participating Cash Value Life Insurance policy. WHOA! You didn't expect that, did you? Yep, good old fashioned Permanent Guaranteed Life Insurance from a mutual life insurance company. That's our alternate bank. As you will see and appreciate, a good agent is indispensable here.

For the record, this is a dividend paying contract with guaranteed premiums, guaranteed death benefit, and guaranteed cash values.

Don't worry, there's no cost to acquiring guaranteed participating whole life insurance. If you are the head of a family, own a business or make long-term financial decisions in any capacity, you want a cash reserve. This is usually a bank account, certificate of deposit, or money market account. You will see that one savings account can be so much more beneficial than having other savings account, IRA's, and non-matched 401(k) plans. It is vital, as you will see, that your money remain both safe and liquid.

Bank Account

Features
- ✓ Pays Interest (taxable)
- ✓ Liquid
- ✓ Guaranteed (if FDIC)

Guaranteed Cash Value Insurance

Features
- ✓ Growth is income tax-free
- ✓ Liquid (usually takes 2 days)
- ✓ Guaranteed cash values
- ✓ Pays annual Dividends
- ✓ Savings in the tens of thousands and even more can be accomplished
- ✓ Positive Leverage (earns higher rate of interest on the dollars leveraged)
- ✓ Great Financing Tool
- ✓ Outstanding cash management system for business and families
- ✓ A high maturity value at death, survivorship benefits for heirs
- ✓ Creditor Proof in Most states
- ✓ Provides "income-tax free" distributions as supplemental income in retirement
- ✓ Supported by Financial Strength of company and State Guarantee Associations

I reviewed many studies providing evidence that the average household debt is a surprisingly high figure with varying degrees of interest charged on purchases and other outstanding debts. There were student loans, automobile purchases, entertainment systems, home improvement costs, and well, you can imagine, the list goes on. In this comparison example, I took three items at various interest charges and averaged them out. Anyone can do this with their own bills at home, just like a business owner should do.

The life insurance is borrowed against to pay off the outstanding debts,

Using Life Insurance Cash Values

	Finance Company	Life Insurance Company
Total Debt	$ 56,000	$ 56,000
Monthly Payment	$ 930	$ 930
Months to pay	84	60.5
Additional Months	24	
Total Cost	$ 78,120	$56,000
Added Cost	$ 22,120	

Considering further that lenders leave you with the product you purchased and no other equity, you would have to be insane not to use the life insurance. Not only have you saved more than $22,000 in payments, but your cash values continued to grow. On that $56,000 you now have more than $72,000 during this period. That's your money, in your account, in your name, not the lenders.

Oh yes, that's crazy, but that's not even the end of the good news. Not only has the balance vanished by using this method, but now you are in a better financial position than would have been possible in almost any other way.

Simply stated, I used a lender loan rate of 10% for the Finance Companies and paid interest on the life insurance side of the ledger with dividends. There was $22,120 saved in payments plus the total growth on the cash values leveraged was $72,000+.

That $56,000 is back in your pocket to be used again if you wish, and you should make that your goal. Plus, you can't ever forget it was growing while the loan was out, your cash value was replenished as you see above, but you also now have the additional $16,000 or more depending on the current rates. That's right, the cash in the policy that was actually borrowed against, **is now worth $72,000+**.

Let's take a straightforward view, only this time from a modified perspective. The numbers are representative only of life insurance policies in force. In this example, dividends are covering the interest.

The Profit Motive

Total Debt	**$56,000**
5 Year Total Payments	**$56,000**
Total Cash Value (growth in your contract) (net of dividends used)	**$72,000**
Net Gain (Gain over debt)	**+$16,000**

What did we do? In this example, you spread your purchasing price out without the interest. You might say that your net cost for the merchandise and services used, it is not $56,000, when applying the 'gain,' it is about $16,000 less. Now from that perspective, that's a 'sweet' spot.

How much sweeter can this get? A lot! How much return did you get so far, by using your life insurance as opposed to not using it? Imagine how far ahead you would be when you do all your financing this way as you go forward.

An important note here. When discussing this with your agent, be sure you understand why in most policies with guarantees and dividends, there is a creative way to use dividends and not have to pay premiums. Premiums can in some cases be cut to just 7 or 8 years or as much as 17 years. The important thing to remember however, is that

Premiums are not continuously required.

Imagine that! We cut our 84 payments down to 60 payments at no additional cost. That saved 24 months of payments. Again,

that's 24 months of no payments due.

Think about that the next time you look at your check book to pay a finance charge.

Could you imagine if you invested your savings and repeated this procedure using rolling five year periods? If you are 40 years old and invested the savings ($22,000) at net, after-tax 5%, every five years, you could accumulate

In 10 years	$ 63,914
In 20 years	$ 191,123
In 25 years @ age 65	$ 243,927

Investing the difference between your own "finance company" (life insurance policy) and the traditional finance companies can make quite a difference in retirement while providing all that comfort in the meantime.

One of the biggest headaches for heirs when someone dies is the deceased outstanding debt that has to be paid off. Guess what, there are two neat features available depending on each one's individual situation.

1) Debt is automatically paid at death through a reduction in proceeds.

2) There is a dividend option that will pay the death claim, plus any dividend additions added to it, plus an amount that covers the full cash value less any loan. Generally referred to as a 'fifth dividend' option. In essence, the loan is paid off through an internal 'term' type rider. The cost depends on age and health.

Get it! It's a win-win scenario. For the owner of the policy, the life insurance is suddenly only 'incidental.' When death does occur, the beneficiary is made whole. You win in nearly every circumstance when proper attention is given to your purchase.

The financial benefits for participating, guaranteed whole life are uniquely strong. It becomes a unique financial weapon.

Whose pocket do you want your money going into, the credit card company or your pockets?

The cash values are a liquid asset, available repeatedly in so many different ways.

This is yet another way of using the difference. When investing the difference, you should check to see what the amount financed would cost you with a finance company or credit card company each month. Compare it to your life insurance policy loan. Have the insurance company set up automatic payments from your checking account, for your life insurance at an amount each month that satisfies the life insurance loan. Take the difference and invest it in mutual funds every month. You and your advisor should agree on the right funds for you. That easy!

One last idea when using life insurance to finance purchases. You have the option to just pay back the principal of the loan and use your dividends to cover the interest. That was one method I used above. You are discounting your purchases. On the down side, you do lose those dividend dollars and the values it would have grown to. Lean on your insurance professional to find what you feel is the best method for you.

Imagine and do the math, what those numbers would explode into if you used your insurance to cover personal loans, department store loans, new roofs, cars and just about anything you would finance.

Think about that business owner that knows how to use cash values as his reserve for his company. He could expand this idea in many additional ways as I will demonstrate later.

This is just one picture of many for an intelligent use of life insurance as a lifetime savings strategy. Using the 'cost' of financing to create wealth is not often an idea you hear, but the concept is more than doable. It makes financial sense. It also makes you feel better when you know you own your own financing company where you are in control.

Before we leave the idea of credit cards behind, there is one more add-on, which you might want to consider. Next time you have to make a large purchase, use your credit card, earn those points, and then immediately pay it off within the interest free period. You are not only saving on interest, now you are getting a bonus as well. Many credit card companies now pay a 'bonus' to you for every dollar you use to make a purchase. For instance, if you use the card and it totals up to $40,000 in a given year, that could be $800 back to you if the bonus were at 2%.

A Word of Caution when using credit cards. You have to think twice before allowing any entity to use your card for prepayments such as toll road payments, coffee and internet services. Once you open that door, it can be difficult to close. Make sure if you do allow this practice that these are bills you can and will pay off monthly. So, choose wisely. Again, credit card use creates loans, not the type you are used to doing, but never forget, these are loans nonetheless.

Pay off all small purchases made with credit cards immediately and never be shy when using your cash values in permanent life insurance to pay off the large balances. Those large balances are the ones you can't pay off quickly. Again, you should meet with your life insurance agent on a regular basis. You want to stay current and 'touch' your money frequently. After all, it's your money and in turn it is your own financing company. You own the contract.

When you put money into a guaranteed, participating cash value life insurance policy, you are taking money out of one pocket and this is important, you are putting it in another pocket. Whatever you think you can do with cash you can do with this policy, after all, it is your money and it is liquid.

No other liquid asset I know of, can provide the possibility of arbitrage in your favor every day. Think of it this way. You are borrowing money from the insurance company at 5% and they use the cash value for collateral, instantaneously. Meanwhile, throughout the process the cash values are growing at 6.5% (which is a variable number depending on the company), you have the advantage of earning a net rate of positive interest.

This is a great way to build outside wealth and/or increase your lifestyle fashion by utilizing permanent, participating guaranteed cash value life insurance. As you will see, these ideas work for everybody who will finance large purchases throughout their life, and we all do. This includes those who would use cash and surrender the future growth of their money.

Here are a few of the additional areas where one can increase wealth with life insurance;

- ✓ Enhancing investment returns
- ✓ Discover why the leading Banks own more than a quarter trillion dollars of cash values, the product they use and why. The companies they prefer and why.
- ✓ Enriching real estate investments designed for cash flow
- ✓ Keeping investment's whole during 'bear' market withdrawals in Retirement

Some of this will be discussed later, but one question does come up repeatedly. How much should I be purchasing. It is a decision to make with a good agent. I like to target the total amount I might want to borrow in about ten years. I would want my cash values to be at least at that amount.

In reality, when using your life insurance while alive, the first consideration is not the death benefit. The first consideration is for how much liquidity you want and when. The decision to target an amount of cash in x years, will produce the premium you need to use. The agent will know how to increase the death benefit if necessary.

One thing to remember however, is the story of the Three Horsemen. They were both happy and they were sad. Your diamonds are in your cash values.

Chapter 4

The Banker

> **"Ideas are a Dime a Dozen
> But the Man that puts them into Practice is Priceless"**
> **Joe Gondolfo**

Working part time in a grocery store while in high school was my first real time job. The starting pay was noticeably good back then; it was $1.75 per hour. I thought I hit a home run. That is, until I got my pay check, saw the federal and state income taxes, union dues and something called Social Security.

That was bad enough, but when I walked in the front door of my home, my mother had her hand out. She wanted half of what I made. No, I wasn't paying rent or sharing in household expenses, for which I was grateful. It was because my father and mother insisted that I was going to start a savings account in a nearby bank. They wanted me to have something to show for my efforts, and to learn how to save to buy the things I wanted.

In the late fifties and early sixties, this was not a unique idea. We held onto the belief that we had to save first and then, and only then, spend. Even though credit cards had been out for a few years, on my part, I wasn't aware that they existed. Looking back, that was the better place to be.

The only problem was that we didn't know we were no better off than the person who used debt to buy whatever they wanted. Financial wisdom was someplace in the background, pretty much like it is today. We hadn't learned the lesson yet. Savings used are savings gone, and that doesn't include the future earning power of those dollars.

Everything you buy, paying cash or using credit, is financed!

At the end of the day when you use credit and pay off the 'loan,' you are back at zero. When you use your own money and make the purchase, that money has gone back to zero.

Using "Positive Leverage" your earnings are at a higher percentage rate than the percentage rate used to borrow against it. If this sounds like something the wealthy and more knowledgeable people do, you are right.

This strategy allows you to take money you have already saved, you use it, you grow it, you use it again and again. Yes, you are borrowing the funds you need, but you are borrowing them from yourself and repaying yourself, all the time your money is growing as if you never borrowed it. The money is always available to you, generally with just a phone call.

When working with a knowledgeable advisor, you can walk through the numerous options available for you. The flexibility of using life insurance for financing purchases is wide. For instance, one could even stop paying premiums a whole life policy after a limited number of years utilizing the dividends in the contract. The cash values can finance loans and you determine the pay back structure you want.

My preference for putting money back into the contract is to pay the same amount the lending company would want for a given number of years. Since this will be more than necessary, it will leave you with many months of no payments. However, as I will repeat, putting those dollars into outside investments such as mutual funds will reward you many times over.

Boy that will explode your rate of return on a life insurance policy! You can't do this all by yourself. You do need the help of a professional and your own representative, does not charge for this service. It should be a part of a regular life insurance review.

What a great financing tool! It's out there and shortly you will learn how anyone can do this. Although different techniques are required because of different circumstances. We will be going through a few of those.

The purpose in the following chart is to demonstrate how the cash value savings continues to grow at a faster pace than any loan made within the contract.

It's about time to check in with the 'Savers.' It seems so righteous to be able to say, "I don't use credit, I pay cash." The thought process is one where we feel good about saving our money to buy the things we want. On the surface, it seems like the thing to do.

However, once we spend those dollars we saved, that money is gone.

Not only is that money gone,
but so are the potential earnings.

In this chart, you can see the savings line grow every year. The savings, called the total cash value, is a straight line, rather than curved to make it easier to understand. It increases every year. The other lines are the loans taken against the cash values every five years.

The Saver family is setting aside $15,000 per year inside their bank savings account to have enough money to purchase their cars. They then spend this money on the cars and now their money is equal to the diminishing value on these cars and gone at the time of trade-in. That's when they begin the process anew starting from scratch

Notice the cash values continue to grow every year, although the surrender value would be reduced by the amount of any outstanding loan.

In this example, the Savers using their life insurance would have $150,000 in total cash values at the end of ten years. They would also have a loan of $75,000, but that leaves them with net cash values of $75,000. That's $75,000 they would not otherwise have.

Looking just beyond that, after twelve years, they would have $180,000 in cash value and car loans (inside the policy) of $45,000. In my view, that's a net $135,000 they now have in their 'savings' account. Again, tell me how much they would have if they paid cash for their cars. Continue following my math, in the fifteenth year inside the life insurance contract, they would have approximately $225,000 with a 'lien' of about $40,000 used for their cars.

The exact amount depends on the policy itself. It's difficult to understand how most of us missed this program over so many years. Yet, there it is. Positive leverage can save a world of hurt, especially when you are in control.

There is a Wrong Way, There is a Right Way

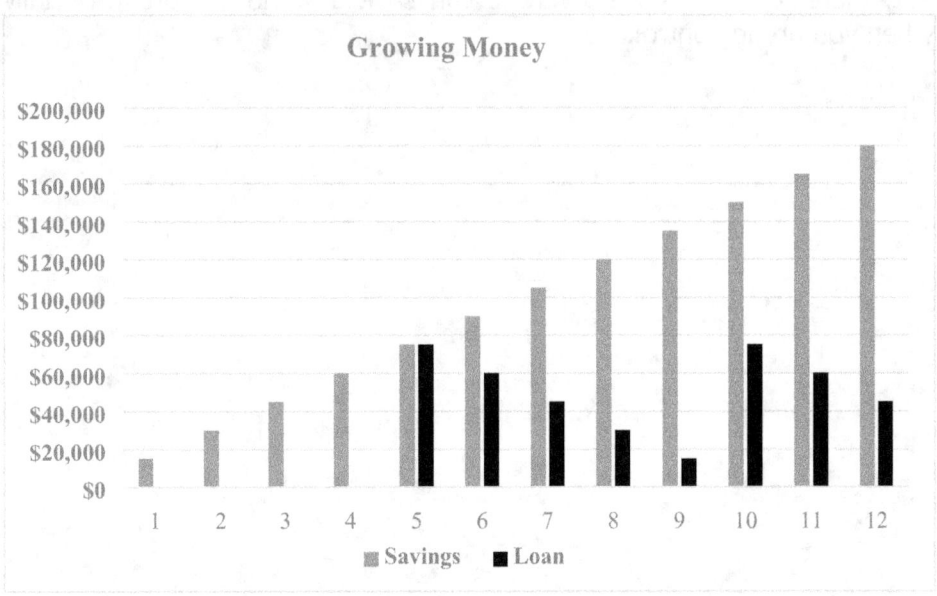

Think about this, the Savers are basically saving their money the same way they did when they used their savings to purchase their cars. The difference is where they put their savings and how they use it.

Isn't that a major point for using guaranteed participating cash value life insurance. The money keeps growing. Almost always growing faster than the lending rate. It doesn't need the stock market to grow, it grows even when the market is down. Wow, and this is available to everyone.

Again, it grows even when the stock market goes down.

It's so obvious why you would use your life insurance as seen in the chart, the benefit of using life insurance over using loans or using your savings. By the way, if you have any other savings or investments that would disappear once used, why would you do that? I can't help repeating myself, the right kind of life insurance is the only liquid asset I know that will keep growing when you borrow from it.

Somebody will interrupt me and say, "but you can borrow against your investments." That's true depending on the registration of an account and the brokerage house rules. However, that's not a solution, it's a problem. The interest rate will be high, you cannot borrow dollar for dollar and very important here, the risk is "high" that you could lose much more than just the amount you borrowed. That happens more often than most investors realize.

Reviewing client accounts recently, I found three different 'loan' rates with the same company. This is not unusual. There is the 'fixed' rate like the 5% that we have been talking about, and that interest rate is a choice of the client. There were also two other current rates on existing client accounts. The options for the owner of the policy generally are 'fixed' or 'variable.'

The fixed is a guaranteed rate that won't fluctuate while the variable will fluctuate depending on economic conditions of the insurance carrier. The variable however, has limitations but a buyer should check it carefully because the choice of interest rate to be paid, once made, cannot be changed.

The two other rates I eyeballed were 3.71% and 4.31%. These are both variable and again subject to change. The client chooses between fixed and variable. The option belongs to the policy owner, not the insurance company and the selection is made at the time of purchase.

How about that? Earning more on their "collateral" than paying for loans against them. True, a residence can do that with an equity loan, but it is not liquid and has fluid conditions. Again, that's No other liquid asset as in NONE! Who wouldn't do it this way other than those who don't know this system exists?

When you call the insurance company service area to borrow from your cash values, there are no credit forms to complete. You can take the money for any reason you want and you don't have to tell the insurance company why you want the funds. You just tell them to send you a check or overnight the money. They aren't going to do a credit check and they don't care if you are working or just lost a job. Why you want the money isn't their concern. The money is on the way to you, the moment they know you are asking for it.

On a recent Wednesday I called my primary insurance company for a loan of a few thousand dollars. How else could I prove my point. I spent approximately six minutes on the phone, and then waited for the check. I waited till 10 am on Friday when the check came via overnight delivery. I immediately deposited it in my checking account and on Saturday morning, the money was available in my account. Wow!

One thing we don't want to do, is to keep giving our money away to the banks and the other lenders, losing it forever. **It's your money**, why not use it while **KEEPING IT**!

BANKS/ Part One

To emphasize the importance of life insurance, it's interesting to learn who is buying extremely large amounts of guaranteed participating life insurance. Doing some homework provided information directing me to giving serious consideration toward our largest financial institutions. Looking at a bank's financial statement then, might surprise you. This is because it surprised me and a few others that work in the life insurance industry. The question then becomes, why do banks own so much guaranteed cash value life insurance?

Banks like many of the features especially the guaranteed and participating parts of life insurance and for many reasons. Some of those reasons include,

- ✓ Liquidity, cash is available
- ✓ Growth Rate, no market losses, goes up every year even when market does not
- ✓ Tax-Sheltered growth, free of income taxes
- ✓ Potential Income Tax Free distributions for providing employee benefits
- ✓ High Contribution Levels for employee benefits, great for executives
- ✓ Key Person Protection, to indemnify bank when brain power is gone
- ✓ These contracts have been in existence for nearly two hundred years and NO one has ever lost a nickel in their contracts. That's true in the face of great depressions, war, and major industry shifts. Banks prefer not to lose money.

I would probably recommend all the reasons listed above for a family or a business as well.

It is my understanding that there are at least 4,000 banks purchasing guaranteed, participating life insurance. It was a curious move for me looking up the total life insurance assets belonging to four banks, two very large, and two that are prominent where I live in the Northeastern part of our nation. The numbers as of September 2018 took me by surprise. (FDIC.gov)

A Compulsive Argument for
Guaranteed Cash Value Life Insurance!

Bank	Cash Values in Life Insurance
Bank of America	$ 22,455,000,000
Wells Fargo	$ 18,617,000,000
PNC	$ 8,518,000,000
T.D. Bank	$ 2,256,000,000

The numbers above represent the life insurance policy's cash values. They do not represent the total face amount that is the death benefit of the policies, which would of course be significantly higher. The total life insurance amounts are generally 5 times or more than the cash values listed above. That's at least a "Trillion" dollars in life insurance.

Well, ok then! In case you are having a problem reading the numbers in the chart above, the cash values are in the Billions of dollars rounded down to the nearest millions. I have been told that Bank executives are supposed to be smart. With so many people saying guaranteed cash value whole life (or a limited pay version) stinks, and saying it in so many ways, why does the Intelligentsia at the banks not only buy it, but buy it in enormous amounts, numbers we have trouble grasping?

Going back fifteen years and recovering the numbers, it would appear that the banks buying the insurance liked it so much, they have continued the trend.

Bank Cash Values in Life Insurance Policies

2004	$ 65 Billion
2007	$ 120 Billion
2018	$ 189 Billion

By the time you look at these numbers, it would be reasonable to assume that **the banks own more than $200,000,000,000 in life insurance policy guaranteed _cash values_.**

The banks own so much life insurance issued by the major mutual life insurance companies that these policies have their own name, BOLI. BOLI simply is Bank Owned Life Insurance. Imagine that! The banks when properly licensed, market almost every asset product available. Yet, only a finite few say anything good about the very brand of life insurance they themselves purchase. It probably stems from sales people at the retail level that prefer the easier sale. The sale that is better for the buyer, takes too much time to educate the consumer who looks at life insurance as something for death only.

I have been in banks often, the same as you. I have listened to conversations about saving and investing, the same as you. Yet, I have never heard a bank representative talk about how useful life insurance is, compared to whatever they are marketing to you at that moment. As a matter of fact, many representatives that sell insurance usually refer to something cutely thought of as 'buy term and invest the rest.' An accepted concept we are putting to rest, as in R.I.P.

There are nearly 6,800 FDIC banks in the United States, and again, more than 4,000 banks hold significant amounts in cash values inside their life insurance policies. What do the banks know that most people are unable to see? It is absurd that there are so many misconceptions about this product, even among many insurance sales people. It may have a lot to do with the blind leading the blind.

Just as an add-on to this conversation; I am stunned as well and horrified that so many insurance agents today, all who went through licensing, are selling life insurance and do not fathom what the products they market are really all about. They don't get the essence of the product. They sell it strictly as a death benefit. The result is we have people being shown how to lose money, by people that should know better, and no one is the wiser, wow!

I have nine children and as of today twenty grandchildren. I want them to understand the importance of a death benefit, but that the death benefit in life insurance is incidental. Because it is so useful during life, I want them to understand why it is whole life, to be used while they are alive, during their 'whole' life.

What's also amazing is how the values of cash value life insurance help fulfill Tier 1 capital bank requirements. Tier 1 capital measures a bank's financial health and can be used when a bank must absorb losses without ceasing business operations. The insurance cash values have in some cases accounted for up to 30% of Tier 1 type capital.

The government too, as indicated above, values the strength of the guarantees in these products, almost promoting it by allowing a percentage of a bank's Tier 1 capital, can be the cash values held by the bank, for satisfying a bank's cash requirements.

First, let's remember that whole life insurance is a multi-faceted tool. While salespeople market it primarily as a vehicle to protect loved ones, many fail to see its daily uses that fit just about whatever financial needs your mind can create. No other liquid savings or investment product offers the unique characteristics and DNA of a good life insurance product. Life insurance contracts should not sit in your desk and wait until someone dies. That would be a foolish use of a very valuable product. That's throwing money away.

I am going to repeat this again, and here goes. When buying life insurance for loved ones, you should NEVER, NEVER, NEVER ask what is the cheapest you can pay for it. I know, this is what so many were brainwashed to think. Instead, you should ask yourself, what is the maximum I can put into a policy?

Term insurance isn't the cheapest form of life insurance.

Term insurance is the MOST EXPENSIVE form of life insurance.

To believe otherwise is to not understand the real differences.

A good advisor can show you using guaranteed whole life, how you are taking money from one pocket and putting into another pocket. It's yours, and readily available. It's still your money, but boy oh boy, how many are the ways you can use it now! What a blessing!

Banks, like the very wealthy, and others who are knowledgeable about these products, embrace cash value life insurance policies, and they use them for many purposes while profiting from them. Shouldn't you be doing the same?

BANKS/ Part Two

When life insurance salespeople make a presentation, they lean on their 'illustration proposal.' Having done that myself, I have at times observed the eyes of the person sitting on the other side of the table, watering up. That's when I recognize that I've lost him. The fact is, that people make up their minds ahead of time and won't let the facts interfere with their decision.

I have for decades shown illustrations to people with all the state insurance required columns included. Nonetheless, I've focused on only three items that are important to people. The three columns I highlight are, premiums, cash values and death benefit. At the end of the day, that's all they care about. The sales person will rush through a presentation hoping to get a message across before the client's eyes say that's enough.

Businesses need cash reserves. Families need cash reserves. Generally, both use banks for their liquidity to meet emergencies or take advantage of an opportunity. However, there is an intoxicating alternative to the typical bank savings accounts or Certificates of Deposit.

Looking at two 'forms' of savings accounts,

	Bank A	**Bank B**
The Guarantee (with limits)	FDIC	by the Institution And through State Guarantee Associations
Rate of Interest (typically)	2%	0% first 10 years Returns, then 2% over next 10 years.
Death Benefit	Savings	Initially 50 times Over deposits
Positive Leverage	No	Yes
Tax-free Growth	No	Yes
Death Benefit Tax-Free	No	Yes
Creditor Proof (by state)	No	Yes
Available Waiver on Deposits	No	Yes

Notes on <u>Bank B</u>:

Rate of Interest for a younger person can be 3 to 5% over 30 years.

Death Benefit is the Life insurance face amount, plus dividends additions.

Positive Leverage: Use CD or Savings Account earning 2% in Bank A as collateral, you get to borrow money from that same bank at a much higher rate of interest.

Life insurance, borrow money let's say at 5% and continue getting 6.5% interest (varies) on the total cash values.

Tax-Free death benefit, Federal Estate Taxes on larger estates is not included here, and there is generally no probate expense or state inheritance taxes due. Obviously, there are no income taxes reportable either. There must be a beneficiary named.

Creditor Proof in nearly all states from bankruptcy and law suits.

Waiver on scheduled premiums in the event of disability. Company makes deposits as if the payer made deposits. All benefits continue to accrue for owner and the beneficiary of policy.

I am making a statement that guaranteed participating whole life insurance doesn't cost anything, it more than pays for itself. Taking another interesting overview of the differences between a bank account or a Certificate of Deposit and Life Insurance.

A young person puts $5,000 away for 8 years into the bank. After 20 years this person stops saving money and doesn't touch his account. At the end of the 20th year, this person's bank statement shows that the deposits totaling $100,000 have grown to $123,920.

The decision is made to withdraw the interest of 2% each year going forward. The withdrawal checks come to $2,478 each year. At the end 30 years after starting the account, the balance remains at $123,920.

Another young person across town has decided to purchase a half million dollars of life insurance for $5,000 per year. After 20 years, there are no deposits to be added. After the 20th year, this young person has $135,610 in the life insurance policy.

In this case a decision is made to withdraw dividends every year. The first dividend withdrawn is for $4,755. The dividend increases each year and in year 30, the dividend withdrawn is for $7,206.

The annual withdrawal in the 20th year exceeds the banks interest paid out of $2,478 by $2,277, and the dividends continue to grow every year while the interest is stagnant.

That's not the end of this story either. At the end of the 30th year, the bank account with interest withdrawn annually, remains at $123,920.

However, the life insurance cash values have grown to more than $205,000 and the cash values in the life insurance will continue to grow.

With greater income, greater cash and the ability to enhance these numbers by using the life insurance to finance your purchases, it becomes a 'no-brainer.'

The Life Insurance over time completely destroys the other tools available for accumulating money. No, **it's not an investment**, as you've repeatedly heard from everyone, **UNLESS you use it**.

An advantage to using a bank account, might be the immediate use of funds through a checking account. The life insurance cash values usually take 2 business days to be made available in your checking account. However, if that is the only real difference, it's insignificant.

When I sit down in front of a married couple or a business owner, I can anticipate the same responses when they know they need life insurance coverage. A breadwinner needs it to protect the family. The business owner requires it for business succession, key man coverage or to cover debts. There are many other reasons as well.

The individuals I am talking with want the "cheapest" form of life insurance they can get, even if it's for a limited time period only. They realize, or most do, that the policy can lapse or run out and they won't receive anything in return.

What they don't know is that they are missing a real opportunity. An opportunity that looks like the exact reasons a bank wants to own permanent, guaranteed participating cash value life insurance. Remember these reasons; they need repeating,

- ✓ Liquidity, cash is available upon request
- ✓ Growth Rate, no market losses, goes up every year even when market goes down
- ✓ Tax-Sheltered growth, free of income taxes
- ✓ Potential Income Tax Free distributions for lifetime income
- ✓ High Contribution Levels for employee benefits, great for executives

✓ Key Person Protection, to indemnify bank when brain power is gone

✓ These contracts have been in existence for nearly two hundred years and NO one has ever lost a nickel in their contracts. That's true in the face of great depressions, war, and major industry shifts.

It is the liquidity factor that can change a life insurance policy into a real investment for some people. In one move, you can improving your current life style, build up valuable assets adding more cash value and simultaneously adding greater death protection for those you love and care about.

Let's take one more example: Borrow $50,000 from a lender at 11% for ten years or use life insurance cash values. Never forget, the life insurance still has a death benefit and continues to grow.

Terms	Monthly Payment	Total Months	Total Paid	Savings Available
Lender	$ 688	120	$ 82,650	$ -0-
Life Policy	$ 530	120	$ 63,640	$ 19,010
Or Life Policy	$ 688	73	$ 50,000	$ 32,650

Dividends were applied to the interest that might otherwise be paid to the insurance policy in the last row. The cash values continued to grow nonetheless. Depending on the age of the policy, there could be significant dividend growth above the use of those dividends used to cover the interest.

Additionally, let's take an overview of what those life insurance policy values that kept growing are now worth. Okay we borrowed $50,000 not from the finance company, but from the policy. That $50,000 borrowed against, over ten years should be worth $75,000. That's $75,000 in your pocket, not going to the finance company.

The take-away here is that you can save serious dollars on financed purchases. You can do this by reduced monthly charges or shortening the payback months.

Then there is the growth in your own money. It not only can cover the interest payments due on financing, but it continues to grow as you earn dollars on the entire amount.

Once you study this concept with your Advisor, how could you not want as much of this product, and at the best premium you can afford, for at least a few years. After at least two years, sometimes even less time or slightly more, you can even begin to leverage the premiums if you find it necessary.

Wow, what better vehicle do you know of where $1 can do the job of multiple dollars? The family wins, a business wins!

Chapter 5

Investments & Retirement

> **"Education is what you get
> from reading the small print;
> experience is what you get from not reading it."**

Earlier it was emphasized that whole life insurance is not per say, an 'investment' in and of itself, unless of course you use it. It is a conservative savings type of account providing a death benefit. I also commented that the death benefit is and should be, 'incidental' to the policy. There are many other benefits that most people would never consider. One unique feature is the ability provided with life insurance to take advantage of other investments.

Enhancing Investment Returns

Earlier I mentioned Kyle Davis, an Advisor working in Florida. He put out an excellent video on YouTube on how one can enhance investment returns. I should add, he did it with caution. I only wish I could imitate his animations here. I thought his 4-minute video contained so much valuable information, I strongly recommend it to everybody.

In a similar fashion, I will attempt to simulate the procedure in which Kyle explained these unique opportunities for investments. Kyle's fascinating presentation, provided his viewers with financial tools that most people did not know exist.

It's important to first point out as Kyle and others have, for longer than I can remember, to state categorically, that using life insurance values for investing may not be in your best interest. All investments carry risk, and your life insurance should be used as a conservative part of your overall portfolio structure, so be careful with this one.

This is a concept that isn't often discussed and for good reason. It can easily be abused if care isn't taken, yet it is an extremely valuable tool when used properly in the world of investments. There are moments that strike unexpectedly and suddenly another opportunity springs itself on us.

My first example happened in 2008 and thanks to the watershed event of homes going 'underwater,' the markets were plummeting. Fortunately, in the office I was working at that time, clients were educated, prepared and made aware that markets could drop precipitously. They surprisingly weren't overly concerned about the markets to call us in high numbers, although a higher number than usual, were making more frequent appointments to do reviews. They had a common-sense attitude toward the market drop and believed the markets were going up again. They understood the mechanics of the system.

My favorite expression when describing the market is that it is like a yo-yo. I've said this before and I'll say it again. It's like a yo-yo, but the whole time the yo-yo is going up and down, it is as if you are walking up a hill. You may not understand how you got there, but at the end of the day you will have significantly more than you started your long trek with.

As a nation we are structured for capital growth, so much so that our government could not in the long run, survive without market progress. They have built their huge entitlement programs around capital growth, and the long-term upward movement in the markets.

Any politician that says they are going after Wall Street and the banks is either lying or dumb. We aren't built to survive without them, and they darn well know it.

This country has so many give-a-way entitlement programs, there is little to no chance of our nation continuing on without a 'little' revolution. I'd refer you back to the writings from our nation's founders for a 'second' opinion on these thoughts, especially Tommy Jefferson who predicted just such an event.

Nonetheless, the one thing that came out of left field back in 2009, was a constant refrain from clients wishing they had money on the sideline to invest in the market because of how much it had sunk. They had an understanding looking at the conditions in 2008 that we were coming back, and why wouldn't we? Nothing was going to hold us back

When markets drop, there are opportunities for investors. Therein too, lies another problem. Most individual money today such as that inside tax-sheltered wraps is already invested. Those wraps are generally their IRA's and 401(k)'s. Thus, very little if anything is available to invest in these moments.

So yes, I mentioned to a few clients that if they were serious, they could use their cash values for investing, and I said it with a warning of the risks involved as well. While no one knows the future, I didn't personally believe any risk of this type was long-term.

Now, before I get in trouble with every regulatory source in this nation, I can't go too far beyond what you see here. However, I'll say it this way. I did my homework and every investor for instance, that would have used $50,000 from their life insurance to invest and hold for five years, would have come out ahead, substantially ahead.

After 5 years, they could have sold out the equity investment account they purchased, paid back the insurance policy loan and the interest due on that loan. Additionally, and according to my calculations, they then could have paid the taxes due on their investment and walked away with $25,000 to $75,000 left in their pocket. That was taking advantage of a bad situation, and it would have been so easy when using their life insurance as a funding vehicle.

Now, let's examine another example, an opportunity where you could place investment dollars. Doesn't matter what kind of investment, it could be for personal or business opportunities as well. In this case, again for personal safety (regulators), I am presenting an out of the box scenario.

Let's say that somehow insanity grabbed hold of our banks, temporarily of course and it wouldn't be the first time. You could suddenly purchase a certificate of deposit, guaranteed to grow at 10% per year for seven years (yeah, I know). In this example the minimum amount to purchase the certificate is $100,000. This is just too good an opportunity to pass over.

You make the call and the insurance company is wiring you the money the next day. A friend tells you he has decided to do the same thing, purchasing a CD from the same bank for the same amount and duration.

At the end of the seventh year, both you and your friend receive notices that your certificate of deposit has matured and will stop earning interest going forward. The amount in the certificates for both of you is identical, $194,872.

You both pay the same taxes due on your gains, and you are very pleased with the results as you should be. Unlike your friend who took his money from his brokerage account, you borrowed it from the insurance company and now you want to pay back the loan and the interest. That comes to $140,710.

	Friend	**You**
Interest Earned	$94,872	$94,872
Taxes @ 20%	$18,974	$18,974
Net Gain	$75,898	$75,898
Plus, Initial Deposit	$175,898	$175,898
Payback Loan + interest	n/a	$140,710
Net Cash Position	$175,898	$35,188

Things aren't looking too good for you compared to your friend, but I'll bet you forgot one little thing, as Kyle would say. The life insurance policy continued to grow as if you hadn't borrowed "against it." In fact, looking at a few contracts and using median type returns, that $100,000 that was originally in your life insurance policy is now worth, $154,380. It is still your own liquid account, available to you at any time.

Now let's take a second look at those numbers after paying off the life insurance loan.

	Friend	**You**
Net Cash Position	$175,898	$35,188
Life Insurance Cash	n/a	$154,380
Total Cash	$175,898	$189,568

Your friend drew his initial funds from his other investments. He was no longer earning anything on those funds. The money was gone, used for this new 'investment.' The life insurance cash values continue to grow whether there is a loan or not. Using your life insurance cash values to fund the investment returned nearly an additional $14,000.

Crazy isn't it how a conservative 'savings' account can outperform by the simple fact that it grows tax-free even when it's being used for other purposes? You have your own win-win scenario.

Once more the difference is known as arbitrage. You are taking advantage of an in-balance in pricing or as in this case, interest differences. As in nearly all cases, the life insurance cash value continued growth wins. A winning combination when mixed into good investment scenarios.

Bottom line, you couldn't lose to your friend while using your life insurance policy cash values, since the arbitrage nearly always favors the life insurance policy owner.

Remember, all investments carry risks, as does the dollar bill itself. Risks include when discussing savings and investments, inflation and taxes. If a CD pays 3% and you are in a 20% income tax bracket, your actual return is 2.4%. Should inflation grow during that twelve-month period at 3%, your now are at a negative 0.6%. A hundred thousand dollars at the beginning of the year would suddenly have a 'real' value of only $99,400. You would be losing purchasing power and not even know it.

Since life insurance is often compared to CD's, I have to ask, "What is the value of a certificate of deposit that can't keep pace with inflation and taxes?"

Yes, life insurance isn't an investment, it's a savings vehicle unless you know enough to use it. I've often heard that

You can make a dollar work harder.
But I think that's wrong.
I would rather make a dollar work smarter.

FROM TIME TO TIME

I had a call recently from a man who worked for the state and he was referred to me by one of his co-workers. I took his call and we had an interesting discussion. He told me that one of his daughters had her wedding day set and he needed $25,000 for the wedding. Not having much money saved, he was told by an Advisor at a bank to remortgage his home to raise the money. Yet, his current mortgage will be paid off in twelve years.

Hearing that I let him talk on and asked a few questions. I learned that he is 58 and would like to retire when he turns 65. He and his wife both work and together have about $100,000 in their retirement plans at work. He also has a pension from the state when he retires.

His debts are limited to his mortgage, cars, and two credit cards with just over $15,000 owed. In my mind I dangled the thought of a home equity loan, but at his age that would be another debt that would probably carry into his retirement. Not something I would want for myself.

As we went over my quick questionnaire, he answered the questions about his assets and liabilities. He mentioned his whole life policy he bought from a large, well known mutual life insurance company. He had been paying just over $740 on an annual basis since he was 21. I asked if he ever used his policy for a loan or made dividend withdrawals and he told me he hadn't. I learned that the original death benefit was for $50,000.

I did a quick mental calculation and if he was correct, that he paid all the premiums and never used his policy, he was sitting on at least $75,000. I asked to see his most recent policy statement and not surprisingly, he did keep his annual "premium" notices. He may not have ever paid attention to them, but life insurance companies put current values on those statements.

His statement showed the current death benefit was $163,000 and the cash values had grown to $84,000. Both those values were well above the guarantees and were due to the annual dividends left in his policy to purchase paid-up additional life insurance. The dividends at that point became guaranteed parts of the contract. He gave me the time to explain how he could use his insurance to pay for his daughter's wedding and pay-off his credit card simultaneously.

If he used the equity in his home and wanted to pay off both the home loan and his credit card over the next 7 years to retire debt free on both, he would have to pay an estimated $770 per month. I explained that by using his life insurance he had a number of pay back options.

Should he want to pay the complete principal and interest back on his policy in like manner, over seven years, which was his choice. The payments on his policy would approximate $546 per month. A clear savings of $224 per month.

A second option might be to let his dividends cover the interest on the loan and he would have more than sufficient dividends to pay future premiums. His total payback would then be just $476 per month and he would save the $740 annual premium as well, reducing his net outlay even further.

He was paying more than $200 per month in credit card interest and $65 a month for his life insurance. Now, if he used the home equity loan and wanted to include paying the credit card off in 7 years, the $200 would be $315 for the credit card and $377 for the home equity loan. A total of $692 each month. That's a few dollars more than the $476 per month he would pay on his life insurance loan. Again, using his life insurance cash values, over the next seven years he would save $18,144 in payments.

I went on to explain to him how the balance of an insurance loan would come out of the death benefit dollar for dollar should he die. He understood that any debt he created outside of the life insurance would still have to be paid and might just come from the life insurance proceeds anyway. You might assume, and correctly, this is less to deal with during a mourning period.

When a few days went by, he called me to thank me. He told me he had called his insurance carrier who went through the numbers with him. He was pleased to learn he could use his insurance to finance his daughter's wedding and pay off that high interest credit card as well. His premium paying days were over as well by using the annual dividends which exceeded his premiums substantially at this point. He was grateful and I was happy for him.

We do get these calls and whenever I can help an individual like this it brings a warm, good feeling. Again, I can't say enough how important it is to have a good, knowledgeable agent who wants to help you and looks at you as his/her client, not as a customer.

In his book, "The Total Money Makeover," Dave Ramsey refers to whole life as a rip-off. Dave Ramsey did not put any application to the cash value other than as a static statistic. What were you thinking Dave?

Perhaps if Ramsey had a good agent educate him, he might now possess the necessary wisdom to share useful information when he opens his mouth. Yet, people listen to, and then act on his 'advice.' That is truly unfortunate.

Failure to understand the living benefits of a whole life type contract can be disastrous to all of us. We have to stop listening to those media personalities who try to sell you on their self-proclaimed brilliance. It's misplaced.

**It only takes a few minutes to learn,
and the rest of your life to enjoy those benefits.**

RETIREMENT

> **"Old age is like an airplane flying through a storm,
> Once you are aboard, there is nothing you can do."
> Golda Meir**

At last you've reached the age you've chosen for retirement. The specific age no longer matters. Today, many people retire because they can afford to do so. Others may decide to put off what would have been their normal retirement age in order to accumulate additional cash as a hedge for the future, while others just couldn't make it if they stopped working. Then there are those like myself, who can't imagine not being productive as long as we have our health and can make, and they do make the good effort and keep going.

Some workers prepared for this day by funding their contributory 401 (k) retirement plan at work to the maximum they felt capable of doing. A few even saved a small 'rainy day' bundle in case it was needed it for an emergency.

Most put so much faith into their plan at work that they failed to take into consideration or accept the fact that they will quite likely increase their spending habits when they are no longer working. For better or for worse, they never imagined that once reaching age 65, they have a better than even shot at making 90 as today's longevity tables are revealing.

Along the way others had even given up enjoying their lives for the sake of saving for the future, only to discover they still don't have what they need or perhaps want. Too many retirees have to change their living habits in retirement, often getting less than what they planned for, because they are afraid of their funds running out.

You may never have believed this day would come, but here it is. Doing your homework, you study the numbers, and you come to realize those statistics saying that the 401(k) accounts will run out long before you die, are more than just frightening. There's no way most accounts are going to work with social security to provide retirees with the true peace of mind they want as they try to replace their current income for the rest of their lives.

You start looking at everything you have, especially where you've spent your money. Turns out you are one of the lucky ones. There is an item that stands out right away. Years ago you bought those life insurance policies to protect your family and you chose the whole life products from that big mutual life insurance company the agent represented, although at the time you thought the premiums were expensive, but also necessary.

You learned early on, how you could use the values you were building up, but you never did. A friend of yours however did, and you learned in discussing your plans with him that he invested the otherwise interest dollars he would have paid on financing purchases and now has another quarter of a million dollars to use in supplementing his retirement. WHAT?

Well, your friends on a roll and tells you how he saved another $400 of monthly premium payments every month by using the dividends in his policy, and now you want your agent to come over and help you make that transition. You are even considering the possibility that you might want to surrender your policies as well. You know you need help reaching a decision. After all, you started buying these when you were 22. That's a lot of years and a lot of money; you don't want to make a mistake now.

During the review the agent listens carefully to everything you're saying. He's particularly interested in what you said about running out of money before you die. He heard you say that you don't want to be a burden to your children. He sits back while you are talking and when you finish there is this moment of silence. You can see the agent's mind is going a mile a minute.

Then he asks you, "Based on what you've learned, how long do you anticipate the money from your retirement plan will last?" You tell him how good a job you've done and that you accumulated $580,000 in your 401(k) and need to take after tax $36,000 – roughly 7.5% out every year.

You also figure that there will be three down markets over the next twelve years and estimate you will run out of money shortly after that. That, plus your savings and social security for you and your wife will help get you through these early years, but once the money runs out, that's another story.

Once again, the agent is quiet, but this time he starts working on his laptop. He needed the laptop to calculate answers that can help you make decisions about your life insurance policies. He starts smiling and says he has an idea, but he's still working that little computer.

When he's finished, he looks at you and says he may at the least have a partial solution. You're thinking to yourself that any solution is good. He continues, and he starts by repeating to you that without making any additional payments, existing dividends structures in your policy will cover all future premiums. That in itself, will reduce your monthly budget.

It's what he says next that catches you off guard. "If your retirement plan runs out of funds after 12 years, you can take $55,000 a year from your policies. That's $55,000 without reportable income, essentially tax-free by using the loan provisions. Not only that, but you will also maintain roughly a million dollars of life insurance for your beneficiaries, again free of income taxes and state inheritance taxes.

He's not done yet. He surprises you with still another option, when he explains how the life insurance values can save your investments during those anticipated bear markets (down cycles). Amazingly, at the end of the cycle, your investment values can be greater than when you started the process. This is one valuable tool, this guaranteed cash value contract.

You remember hearing a few times about taking income from your policies in retirement, but it never captured your attention. It was too dry and boring at that time.

You can't thank your agent enough and when he leaves, you feel so much more relaxed about your future.

It was nice of him to show you how you can improve your cash position in retirement. Knowledge is a wonderful thing. You learned,

a) How to cover holes in your investments when the market crashes.
b) How to use your cash values to supplement your income, tax-free in your later years.
c) A reminder on using your cash values to enhance your current lifestyle any your lifestyle in retirement.
d) Leaving a legacy for your loved ones regardless of market conditions and your investment balances.
e) How to protect your IRA from the ravages of taxation.

Your rate of return while good for a conservative vehicle hasn't been spectacular on the polices that are earning about 2% to 4%. However, that continuous net growth even when there are loans out could have been used making the policy that more valuable.

In some ways the peace life insurance can bring you, may actually contribute to keeping you alive longer according to some data I had looked at years ago. That's some kind of physiological thing. One more item to help your attitude,

Stop thinking about Life Insurance as a Death Benefit

A Bear Market in Retirement Can Put Future in Jeopardy

In the preceding paragraphs I mentioned that guaranteed life insurance contracts can help you protect your investment assets in 'down' markets. There are a few insurance companies that now support this idea with booklets showing exactly how this can be accomplished.

The MassMutual Life Insurance Company recently put out a booklet called "Taming a Bear Market in Retirement." Shortly after I first saw this piece, other insurance companies followed with their own versions. However, I am referring to the MassMutual because as you will see, they are on my own short list of preferred companies. You should get your hands on a copy of it. However, I will use my own approximate numbers along with the general concept so you can get a feel for this intriguing and useful way to preserve your investments.

The companies promoting it use an example such as having $800,000 in an IRA. The IRA owner decides that $60,000 per year is to be drawn from that account. That in addition to social security adds up to a nice income for a husband and wife to live on throughout retirement. In our example, the advisor's clients, Frank and Betty listen intently. The advisor tells them, this is a higher percentage allowance than he would recommend, but they insist.

The advisor believes however, that Frank and Betty can still achieve their goals since they desire to reach higher than many others in retirement. He takes out a copy of "Taming a Bear Market in Retirement," and he replaces the numbers to fit Frank and Betty.

He explains if they had retired twenty years earlier pulling out that same percentage for their income, their current IRA values of $800,000 would have been reduced to less than $250,000 today. In only another five years or so, there might very well be nothing left. This unnerves them a bit. The agent explains how they can protect themselves. In fact, they are fortunate to be in a position to apply the techniques immediately should they need to do so.

The advisor than demonstrates to them how they could use funds from their cash value life insurance policy in the four or five down years anticipated over the next twenty years to make up the difference. Since they are in a twenty percent tax bracket, they need only borrow $48,000 to continue the same after-tax level of income. The advisor explains this procedure in such a method that Frank and Betty can easily see and appreciate how this concept works

Over the twenty years they could take four income tax-free loans or more, but in this case the total would be $192,000. This keeps their spendable income level. Yes, of course they are required to continue making 'Required Minimum Distributions' from their traditional IRA. However, in this situation, these distributions need to be immediately flipped into non-qualified investments (meaning investments outside the IRA).

Keeping your investments invested, will allow for the re-capture of your account balances prior to the bear market. The life insurance cash values you have can carry the burden providing the income you need during these 'down' markets.

Again, in the bear market years, they take the IRS required amount, pay taxes on that number, and reinvest in a 'non-qualified' account. This separate account is theirs to do anything they want with the money in their new account which of course, would probably be used for income.

At the end of the twenty-year example, illustrating what happens when using life insurance to fill in the holes created by the down market, they make an evaluation. Now they examine their combined Investment 'accounts,' the IRA and the money outside the IRA, and they get a big surprise. The combined accounts may now be worth as much as two million dollars. Quite a surprise, very manageable and quite noticeably higher than a quarter of a million dollars.

That's right, a good possibility it would be nearly two and a half times more than they started with. Add in the policy cash values, which are still growing, and now the concerns they had earlier have changed to smiles on their faces.

As the advisor continued to explain to them the method he utilized, they began to grasp an entirely new approach on using their life insurance. Until this time, they thought of it primarily as a death benefit, not having understood the many creative uses the insurance could have on their lives.

Like many others, they were learning what the "whole" in whole life insurance really means. It is to be used during your lifetime as well as for your surviving heirs.

The advisor had another benefit to share with them, a different route if desired. The loans from the life insurance don't have to be paid back. The dividends are strong enough, and have been for a long time, to cover all the interest due on the loans and even begin attacking the loan principal. Meanwhile the cash value can continue doing its thing, it will keep growing.

Their permanent cash value life insurance has become even more important to Frank and Betty as they were discovering new uses available to them. Using it for things they never previously imagined. Heck, they learned how they could even use their insurance for financing purchases, down payments on a condo and vacations. These two began developing a real love relationship with their permanent life insurance. Who would've thought?

Enriching Real Estate Investments

This is for those who prefer to invest with income producing real estate. It's fair to say that these investors feel they can reach their financial goals much faster than others who invest in stocks and bonds, usually through mutual funds. If they didn't believe this, they wouldn't take the risks.

In some cases, they are right. However, too many fail to see and understand the obstacles they face and their subsequent losses can be torturous. The fall-out can be avoided with the necessary education, due-diligence, discipline and a solid structure to build upon.

There are many benefits to those who are successful when it comes to investing in income producing real estate. Some of the principal benefits include,

a) Appreciation in the property
b) Equity between value and mortgage
c) Leverage to use the equity to acquire additional properties
d) Cash Flow from the after expense rental income
e) Inflation hedge since real estate for more than a hundred years has moved along the same curve as inflation
f) Tax-advantaged, and this you should be careful and I urge those who take this advantage to set-aside those dollars saved this way. For most, there will be a day of reckoning.

Best results for financing and purchasing income producing real estate generally requires using Other People's Money (OPM) to invest in these ventures. While some investors are not aware of this, wealth acquired this way is highly dependent on the amount and kind of financing utilized. It may be the single most important aspect among others, when purchasing investment real estate.

Forty years ago, real estate investors were able to obtain zero down mortgages. That's no longer the case. Today's world requires a down payment that can range from as low as 10% down and upwards of that number. There are many factors that go into the bank's reasoning for lending money on real estate, and determining down payments and final interest percentage.

There are many strategies involved in getting the necessary start-up funds. Once this is accomplished however, the initial moves made by the investor can be exploited many times.

Ok, so Dave has decided that he wants to get his share of the wealth and he is willing to take what he perceives as the necessary risks involved. A small multi-tenant property he is looking to buy will cost a half million dollars and the bank he is working through wants a 20% down commitment. That translates into his needing to coming up with $100,000. Not exactly what he had stashed aside in his piggy bank.

Dave might need to look elsewhere for that initial deposit. This usually comes in the form of peer to peer or corporate financing. Either method requires payback plus interest. That payback as well as the interest required is going into someone else's pockets.

Money for a down payment can also come from a number of sources such as savings, investments, borrowed out of tax-qualified retirement accounts, using home equity loans or other, available financing sources.

No matter where the money comes from, there's going to be a cost, and it is generally a non-recoverable cost. If he were to take the money out of savings or investments, not only is the principal gone, but also his future earnings from that money are gone as well.

If financing comes from a qualified retirement account like a 401(k) or an IRA, it could also cost a large amount for taxes. Not only are the income taxes going to be due, but so is a penalty tax if he is under 59 and a 1/2. Make sure you've spoken with an advisor or accountant before using monies from a tax-sheltered retirement account.

As an example, should Dave be able to grow his money at 5%, he would double it in about 14 years. That's lost money and a large consideration before entering into any transaction, because that is the money he is giving up. In essence, he is giving up at least $2 for every $1 he uses for this new venture, that carries it's own unique risks. This should compute into his final calculations as either a 'go' signal or a 'stop' signal.

I would think that payment(s) with interest, are probably commensurate with the risk. No matter where it comes from, that finance money is going to the lender.

There are methods investors use to recover start-up money quickly. One popular strategy is to buy depressed property compared to the surrounding structures in that vicinity, fix it up sufficiently to increase the value of the property and refinance in a method that recovers the original deposits. A great concept when it works.

Most real estate investors seek tax advantages, passive income, growth and would prefer their investment be untouchable by creditors if possible.

Dave went ahead and purchased the property borrowing the down payment from his family. They were generous with the interest rate when lending him the capital he needed. After all, it's family.

Sixty months later, Dave wanted to know how he made out on his investment. He brought his accountant in and they crunched the numbers. Turned out he and his money did well. When Dave and his accountant computed the return on the initial $100,000, it came out to be a hair over 15.5% for each year and Joe felt great about his decision to make the purchase.

Dave's accountant went further and looked at Dave's IRA return over the same period. He did well with his IRA as well as he earned just over 7% each year. Dave definitely made out better with the real estate, but it was the riskier of his investments and provided him with the ability to experience angina from time to time.

Dave's $100,000 (the money he borrowed) has returned him $105,546 (net) over his initial investment. That's a return anyone would have liked, and that's after paying back the money he borrowed from family. This includes paying the loan back, expenses, any taxes paid and takes into account his significant tax deductions as well.

Those dollars Dave initially used was viewed as the price of doing business. To summarize, if borrowed, he has to pay back the interest and the principal at some point. If he used savings or investments, that money is gone forever.

Let's turn the table a bit and say Dave had that money in his life insurance cash values. That he borrowed from his life insurance and made the same payments back as he would his family. What would have happened?

A number of positive things would have happened, mostly in Dave's favor and he would have had an even better feeling. When Dave paid back his lender, that money disappeared as it should, into the lender's wallet.

If Dave had used his life insurance to bank his venture, he would have improved those numbers making up his rate of return, and it would have been dramatic.

- ✓ Dave could have created his own terms using the life insurance loan provision. He could have skipped all payments on it until the end of the investment cycle, paid it all (principal plus interest) at a given point down the road, perhaps waiting to sell the property, or paid some or all of the interest along the way. He could have paid back the principal while letting his dividends cover the interest and pay down the loan. It would have been his call.

- ✓ Yes, he could have waited until he sold the property and at that point replaced the loan plus the interest, and he would be ahead of any other method because of the positive arbitrage built into the life insurance. The life insurance values would have continued to grow and he has that money to use again.

✓ Using his life insurance would have increased Dave's average rate of return by a hefty amount. Based on my numbers, he could have realized an average rate of return much greater per year, had he used the life insurance to finance his down payment. I have seen other numbers on the Internet experienced by others which claim it would have more than doubled his return over the first ten years.

How about that! Unlike using almost any other financial vehicle, Dave's cash value would have continued to grow, even with the outstanding loan, thanks to the growing guaranteed cash values and dividends being paid.

In essence, Dave had the real estate working for him and could have the life insurance working right alongside his investment. He would have two pillars of strength, one being the money inside the real estate and non-liquid; the life insurance monies growing with guarantees and tax-sheltered. Lest I forget, he might also have his emergency funds in his policy. The best combination of two worlds working for you.

Earlier I said that the life insurance portion of the contract is incidental. Well, it is, but a widow without it might not look at your real estate investment loan in a supportive way. Your spouse is well aware of the high debt on the property or properties. No one wants to worry about those at your death. The life insurance gives them a bridge over time to, and if they wish, to sell the properties.

Best practices plus a bank's requirements, often point out the need for life insurance. A bank can and will call in a loan when the borrower dies. Without life insurance, the widow will have a large non-liquid asset, suddenly a potential liability, with no immediate cash to pay off the mortgage.

Banks understand this dilemma and especially in these circumstances, they want their money. In some instances, banks actually require the purchase of life insurance or a lien against existing life insurance policies. This remains a smart business practice for banks, and one you don't want to fool with. It actually can be a benefit both parties.

Let's review those principal benefit bullet points for investing in real estate.

    a) Appreciation in the property
    b) Equity between value and mortgage (loans)
    c) Leverage to use the equity to acquire additional properties
    d) Cash Flow from the after expense rental income
    e) Inflation hedge since real estate for more than a hundred years has moved along the same curve as inflation
    f) Tax-advantaged, and this you should be careful and I urge those who take this advantage to save those dollars saved this way. For most, there will be a day of reckoning.

As I read them, they look strongly like life insurance, but with a better Internal Rate of Return. But it is the life insurance that can and does enhance the returns on real estate. Life Insurance adds a couple of other benefits as mentioned, and these major points immediately come to mind;

    a) A much greater death benefit
    b) Creditor proof
    c) Emergency cash for maintenance

As a final note, anyone involved in commercial real estate should be aware of the significant tax-benefits at the time of sale utilizing Section 1031 of the Internal Revenue Code which will allow for the deferring of taxes due and provide greater cash flow on the sale of qualifying properties.

There are a few stringent rules to follow, but nothing that can't be easily met. The best advisors for the property owner to use include, but are not limited to,

    a) A Commercial real estate broker
    b) An Accountant that understands the rules involved with Commercial Real Estate
    c) A securities Broker who is familiar with the ins and outs of Section 1031 and may have replacement properties available through a securities type structure.
    d) A lawyer who works with Section 1031

All of these advisors can add an important element for real estate investors. If one presidential candidate at the time used this part of the code to eliminate taxes, we should respect, not despise him for having done this successfully.

Life insurance is just as useful in the financing end of investment real estate as it is to enhance investment returns.

Chapter 6

Business Owners and Others

> **So you put something away for a rainy day**
> **And it's an umbrella**

While this chapter is aimed toward business owners and their situations, most of the life insurance applications for businesses are also applicable to the family. Some are evident, others not so obvious. The only difference I have noticed over the years are the number of zeros. A business will often deal in the millions of dollars, while families are targeting the hundreds of thousands.

The business owner knows there is a serious need for life insurance coverage. There are obligations, debts, and promises to be kept, including those promises made to the owner's own family. Life insurance fulfills those needs should the owner die. It takes a silent stress away from a responsible business owner.

A life insurance agent walks into the office of an owner running a small business. They both know why they are there. They have previously discussed business succession. The owner would like his heirs to successfully take over. Sitting on the other side of the table, the life insurance agent wants to help the business owner and of course, he wishes to make a sale.

This should be a simple, what does it cost, write it up type of meeting, but it's far from that. While the business owner has pre-determined, based on everything he knows, that term insurance is cheap and the way to go, the sophisticated life insurance agent knows better.

But there is an obstacle to overcome. He has to get into to the business owner's mindset. Stubbornness can make for bad decisions.

Instead of getting right into the proposal, the agent goes through a review of questions previously asked to acknowledge the information given at their last meeting. One of the key questions asked and in a routine fashion is, "How much do you keep in your cash reserve?"

The owner replies to the agent's question and says that the company keeps approximately $300,000 in reserve. That along with a diminished cash flow is about 6 months operating expenses. It includes the salaries of his key people, and the essentials needed to run the business in the event the bottom fell out.

"Very nice," the agent thought to himself. The agent knows that every business and every family should keep a strong cash reserve for emergencies in particular, and also for any opportunities that may arise. He was happy this owner was following a blueprint with good business practices.

If the agent heard that there was no cash reserve, or that the cash reserve was insufficient, the next few minutes would have been spent discussing the needs for having one. In this case, there was no need to go over those reasons for being prepared for an emergency or opportunity.

The agent skillfully going through his questioning, learned that the cash reserve is held in cash inside the company's brokerage account with an investment firm. The owner tells the agent that his broker is always trying to get those dollars out of cash and into the market, but that brings worries the owner doesn't want. Zero percent is better than a down market at a time the business may need those dollars.

The agent learns that the owner is okay with the fact that the real advantage to the cash reserve is preservation and liquidity. Knowing that they both agree on that point; the agent goes through an illustration on why the whole life being proposed is a good buy. However, the owner is fixed on what appears to be the high cost. The owner already had an idea what a twenty-year term policy might cost and this proposal seems extraordinarily high.

The agent was prepared for that so there is a sheet showing the owner the benefits. First explained that the owner is not giving up any money, just creating another, more productive cash reserve. The owner would be moving funds over time from one cash reserve to another. Just like moving money from one savings account in a bank to another savings account in a different type of bank.

As this business owner is about to find out, moving money from one pocket to another has many advantages. This new reserve carries the life insurance needed for the owner to pay off any company debts, reimburse the owner's family with the full value of the company, and leave the remnants of the company, both good and bad to the family. This removed any major concerns, since they would have already received the value for the company from the insurance company.

Additionally, the agent demonstrates the value of this new reserve system, using it as the owner's own finance company. Any distributions are not obstacles to the reserve's growing values and will save the owner considerable financing cost going forward.

The owner studies this suggestion on creating the company's own financing program, by using the cash values of a guaranteed participating cash values life insurance policy. He particularly likes the option that once the policy is established, if necessary, dividends can pay all interest charges while the company pays back the pure dollar value of the loan. Thus, one way to discount his larger purchases.

He also liked the fact that his dollars were going back to himself and any loans on the policy when used for financing would not show up on any credit reports. He also thought out loud, that the policy values were increasing without having to report any earnings to the government. He felt his taxes were more than generous anyway.

Turns out that even with the reserve, the company is currently paying a heavy amount of interest every month on company loans. The owner never realized that life insurance could reduce the cost of running the business. No one ever told him how he could use the values tucked into the life insurance policy. You can see the owner's eyes going from red when hearing the premium, to money green as the realization of the living benefits of life insurance were coming into play.

The agent wasn't done. He wanted to bring up what some may consider a 'large problem' that wasn't yet in the discussion. The agent explained that there is a blueprint to follow to ensure that life insurance proceeds remain free of income taxes. The agent slides into this and explains that while there is a problem, there is a solution. The business owner appreciates his help.

Months later after the policy is issued and the owner reflects on this, he knows he has made a good financial move. He even feels morally good knowing he has fulfilled an obligation of taking care of those he loves, for whom he is the economic lifeline.

The Bicycle Shop

This is ancient history for many of you since it happened in the 1970's. I love this story and have told it numerous times over the years.

I was referred to the owner of a new bicycle store in Philadelphia. When I first walked into the shop at the appointed time, and shortly after he met me, he stated emphatically, "I'm not interested in life insurance."

I was still new at the time and he caught me off guard. It might have been the only moment in my life that I was tongue-tied. Trying to grab my thoughts, I pointed to, and asked him about a bike. He immediately went off into a sales pitch, but it gave me the pause I needed to respond to his initial comments.

There was a story running around in my head, and I made a decision to use it. I'm not here to sell you life insurance. I represent a company that would like to buy your store at a specified time in the future, and we will give you a contract to do just that.

Can I ask, if you were to sell, how much would you want for the store?" He thought about it and came up with, $150,000. Taking a pad out to write down notes, I said, "We'll do that. First thing, should you die, this company will pay your heirs $150,000. However," and now I am making bullet point notes on my pad, "There are a couple of conditions to do this." He was listening intently. I am sure I was the first person to ever approach him like this.

"As a show of good faith, my company will want you to open up a 'banking account' and deposit $4,000 into it every year for the next ten years. The account will have your name and only your name on it. You can use those dollars for anything you want at a small charge.

The company I represent is one of the top ten financial institutions in our country. The money in the account is yours to use. If after ten years, or actually at any time, you want to break the contract, the company will refund you your money.

Should the time come and you retire, you can use our contract to take income that is tax-free, to supplement any other retirement dollars you have coming in.

Now, should you die, your wife does get the full $150,000 plus interest left in the contract. Additionally, thanks to a quirk in the contract, she or your heirs, get to keep the store and run it or sell it and anything they get is in addition to our buy-out."

He didn't hear another thing. He pulled out his checkbook and asked for the application to sign. He also guessed it was life insurance and he said, "I've never heard it explained this way before. I can use the life insurance to buy bikes from the manufacturers, use the dividends to cover interest for holding the bikes until such time as they are sold, and effectively increase my profits. Even more importantly, my wife won't ask me anymore what happens to her and the shop should I die."

He didn't want to buy a drill. He wanted the holes a drill makes. That's the story of life insurance. No one wants it, they just want all the things it can do for them.

"Split-Dollar"

In another business situation, which again applies to the family, a business owner wants to provide a benefit for a key employee. He doesn't want to lose this person who has proven valuable and loyal to the company. He would like to provide protection for the employee's family and add to his retirement income. Money in this company however, is tight.

The agent in this scenario is offering the owner a program to provide all of this to the key person at almost no cost. In fact, he emphasizes that the company can provide all of this with a new type of "savings" account. In this account, the owner deposits (ok, premiums) with the corporate name on the account as owner.

The owner immediately has use of about 90% of the deposit if needed. This account will also provide financial protection to the keyperson's family and, when the time comes, will provide supplemental retirement income to the keyman. This second benefit however, will depend on how many years the employee stays with this company.

Amazing, because the company has use of those funds for the next decade or so and, should the employee die, the company will receive back all of it "deposits" at 3% interest. Wow, nobody loses. We have nothing but winners.

The owner further learns that there is a small tax, and I mean small, on the part of the premium attributed to pure insurance for the outside (the company) beneficiary. Wow, a double winner because that 'small, supplementary' amount is what gives the pure insurance to the owner's family with all the tax advantage not otherwise available.

The agent asks if there are any questions and of course, the business owner has questions. When they are finished, the owner looking at all the numbers and how to use the life insurance changes from,
'What is this going to cost me'
to,
"How much and how soon can we begin transferring funds to this new account?"

If the owner didn't have a cash reserve at the start of the discussion, there would have been a desire to have one at the end of their meeting.

I really love this business. I can help people in very creative ways, help their families, help charities, and others simply because I understand both the living and the death benefits of life insurance, and yes, the agent is essential to guide the process.

As for the business owner (or family provider) discovering this innovative way to use life insurance on a regular basis while alive, the business owner now knows,

**"The life insurance doesn't cost anything.
It's like a 'free' benefit.
It's just using a different, and a better pocket to put my
reserve money."**

As we will see this concept used somewhat differently when discussing its use by a family, the end results, these benefits are there for all to use. There are many other uses of Split-Dollar and we will go through a few examples.

We forget that Professional offices are businesses too, whether everybody recognizes that or not. If professionals fail to run their practices as a business, the doors will close. The professional will be looking for work under someone else. Like a businessman, the professional wants to increase the projected stream of income at retirement.

To have funding for additional retirement income, when knowing how to apply it to so many financing applications makes this one very valuable asset on the balance sheet of any business.

The Top Hat Program

This is a routine question that those in our industry frequently heard coming from successful business owners, accountants and others as well. I've 'maxed out' my retirement plan, but need to put more away. How can I do this?

First as a suggestion, a review of the benefits of a tax-qualified retirement plan as they appear to you. Usually, those asking that question want the income tax-free growth of a plan and if it's a traditional plan, the tax deductions for contributions. If it's a 'Roth' type plan, the real tax-benefits come from income tax free distributions.

The problem with layering another plan on top of what they already have, is usually contribution limitations and governmental controls, plus the recognition of the need of that third party administrator and inclusion of other required costs.

There is one product that fits this need quite handsomely and gives many, numerous other advantages to the owner of a company. It's a 'non-qualified' plan using life insurance, and my favorite contract is with a mutual life insurance company called, (yeah, you can help me say it) guaranteed, participating whole life insurance.

There it is, the life insurance for a company represents,

a) A benefit to the owner's family
b) A benefit for the company
c) A benefit for your own financing company
d) A benefit for key man protection
e) **A BENEFIT FOR TAX-FREE RETIREMENT INCOME**
f) One dollar, doing the work of many

If I asked you what runs through your veins, you would tell me it's your blood. If I asked a business owner what runs through his/her veins (the business), they might also answer blood. Those who do would be wrong. Capital runs through their veins, and that blood can be healthy or weak depending on the reserve capital.

Business owners are busy either selling their products or managing the business. New entrepreneurs quickly discover that both skills are required to be successful. They do it day to day and while looking ahead only for a month or two, they may be satisfied that everything is ok. However, that's not always the case.

Running a business requires a long-term outlook, and long-term means there's going to be a need for cash at some point, and that time will come, just as it does for a family. The source of that need is different for each business and industry. They will either finance projects themselves or look for Other People's Money. Doing it the way described here, at least for me, is the greatest savings account one can have.

Now, before you attempt this maneuver to help you prepare for retirement, check it out first with your accountant. Let's say you want,

a) An informal retirement plan either outside of a qualified plan or in addition to one with the least amount of government involvement.
b) You want to put away a larger amount than permitted in a qualified retirement plan.
c) You don't want to use outside administration, nor do any paperwork.
d) You want to grow assets without paying taxes on the growth.
e) You want the money liquid in case you need it.
f) You want the asset to grow even when borrowed against.
g) You want to borrow money against this asset at a lower rate of interest than is being earned.
h) You want this retirement 'plan' to be fully funded and tax-free to your heirs.
i) It's important you also get tax favored savings after putting your dollars into this plan.

There are many more uses for business owners and for those who don't own businesses. The more you learn about using whole life insurance for your daily and future needs, how can you not get excited about it?

There is just one more view for business people referred to as an "Executive Bonus Plans" using Section 162 of the IRC. So long as your compensation is "fitting" and not overabundant, your business can pay a key man's life insurance premiums and deduct the 'expense.'

That means the executive must pay taxes, but on a reduced amount of income necessary for the premium. The executive owns the policy including the cash values. In this simplified example, you can see the benefits.

If the premium to the executive is $20,000, the executive would need to earn $28,571 before tax. The company would have to pay that $28,571 plus the ancillary expenses necessary. If these costs came to 30% of payroll, the employer would have to pay a total of $40,815.

Using an Executive Bonus arrangement, the company could pay the premium and expense it out at $20,000. The executive would have to claim the bonus and pay taxes of $6,000.

The Executive Bonus arrangement just saved the company and the executive thousands of dollars. It does so as it goes forward every year.

In this example there is an overall annual savings of more than $14,000 and get this, it gets even better. This executive is just like you. During a review with his insurance agent, he learns how to use his life insurance cash values to reduce the cost when financing purchases. This savings in turn can be used to more than cover the taxes he pays for the insurance premiums. The executive makes an even greater profit. Wow!

We're not done yet! Let's see what happens at retirement. The executive has a life insurance contract with cash values, let's say now worth $450,000. The executive can in most cases start borrowing from this policy $2,000 every month income tax-free. The policy will stay in effect, but the face amount will fluctuate due to the use of loans that reduce the death benefit dollar for dollar. Dividends meanwhile are adding death benefit amounts to the life insurance to cover some or all of the loan, especially beneficial to the executive's family.

If our executive delayed taking the withdrawals until another five to seven years go by for instance, the executive might get close to $3,000 each month income tax-free using the policy loan provision. Talk about one dollar doing the work of many. This is true whether the policy was used for financing purposes or not.

If our executive uses the insurance in retirement mode for financing and income, the benefits actually can increase. Paying back the "lender" costs of financing, increases the cash value, and that in turn strengthens the income available. Just think what you can do with the help of a knowledgeable life insurance agent.

In this Scenario

A company, I will call 'Space' was working with NASA more than four decades ago and sought to solidify its relationship. NASA contracts provided Space with its marginal profits every quarter and to lose this business would have been a blow to this company.

One day the owner of Space found out that the balance sheet had to improve to obtain long-term, guaranteed contracts from NASA. The owner knew the need for an immediate infusion of Capital to improve sales and in turn, improve the bottom line.

The company owner put together a good business plan and presented it to the bank for a loan. Initially, the request was refused. After a few weeks of negotiations, the bank agreed to lend the money but at a high rate of interest. The interest rate was an obstacle, and there weren't any other options, the owner would have to settle for it.

Then the surprise, the line of credit requested required life insurance on the owner to be assigned to the bank to cover the loan. The good news was that the owner had the loan. The bad news was that at the owner's age and with a few health issues, there were problems to address. The owner informed his agent that the coverage for the loan was needed yesterday. The owner wanted to do it fast in case the bank changed its mind.

The owner had a medical history with a bad heart. The agent worked on the medical problem with underwriting at a number of insurance companies and did manage to bring in a decent rating. If you call two times the premium quoted for the term coverage a good rating. Nonetheless, the owner had no choice and was forced to accept it.

The owner was previously warned over many years that one day the need for life insurance would present itself. This was one of the ways the agent envisioned. The owner kept putting off the purchase because this was one person who was immortal and felt there would never be a need for it. All those stories that he would not need life insurance turned out to be lethal. The need for insurance, his age and his health cost a lot more than ever anticipated.

The multitude of reasons for business life insurance never cease to amaze me. I was working at my desk when what seemed to be a frantic call came in for me. It was an associate, a friend from New York and he told me he needed a few minutes of my time, he needed my help. He asked if my primary insurance carrier would split cases with other carriers. Would we join in to provide sufficient coverage for someone requiring more than most companies would issue on one life.

Now this call came a few decades ago and 'jumbo' type policies weren't issued as they are today, due to many risk factors. The risk for a single company could be huge, a quick death and for the amount of coverage wanted here could give an insurance company a bloody nose.

I told my friend that I would have to check if I could participate after he gave me the key information I would need. Turned out that the life insurance was needed for a major television entertainer and nearly ninety million dollars of coverage was wanted.

The television network wanted participating, guaranteed life insurance for potential lost revenues should this man die. They also wanted the contract to fund a number of items including paying the entertainers' widow, bringing in a replacement, supporting promised deferred benefits to the entertainer and of course, replacing lost revenue. The network also understood the benefits of having a big cash reserve on hand and using it, while maintaining all the other benefits as well.

The agent making the presentation also showed the network another method of purchasing a policy. The premiums could be financed 100% by a bank and paid back through the cash values or financed after the first year, partially by the policy itself. These are more common practices than are generally known, especially where premiums are up in the stratosphere.

Man, I was excited, but thankfully not too much. As things worked out, the life insurance didn't require more than three companies working together and my friend was thinking it would be more. I was surprised that so much coverage was wanted on one person, even though this personality drew extremely high television ratings. Sadly, I wasn't needed.

The network knew the importance of the potential liabilities should this man die. The risks were high and they wanted to know they had their backs covered. Key man protection for them was high in their priorities as it should be for all businesses.

Like banks, they knew that life insurance is an economic powerhouse, and when structured properly it is a tremendous financial weapon. The network's priorities were key man protection, reserve capital (liquidity), protection for entertainer's heirs and supporting his retirement.

In another event, I had one client who owned a new car dealership. He repeated a particular practice every November. When I first introduced the idea of his purchasing key man policies on his key people, he was interested and we had a few meetings before he agreed to go ahead with the purchase. It turned out that liquidity was more important to him than I had realized from our previous discussions.

It ended with him taking out large cash value life insurance policies on his three key employees and at the time of purchase, he insisted that these be strong cash value contracts. A couple of years went by and in one mid-November he called and asked that we send him a check for $100,000 from the policies. He had his money within days, he called and thanked me. I never asked what it was for, even though my curiosity was always present. Before I got to see him again, in mid-January, he sent the money back with a tiny interest payment. This procedure followed for a number of years with the amount he requested growing each time.

One day during a routine review, my friend drew me aside and he thanked me. Not having any idea why he was thanking me, I asked him to explain his gratitude.

He told me that every year during the first week of January, the auto manufacturer he represented audited his bank accounts. They always wanted to know his financial strength, by going through his cash accounts, and they would want to see that the money was there for a full thirty-day period.

He used the cash values to cover any amounts they might otherwise think as insufficient. He deposited the cash value loans into his bank account and let it sit there. I tried to explain that the cash values in these policies were about as good as cash he had in the bank. That they would accept it as a cash equivalent, but he preferred doing it his way.

He went on to tell me he never forgot my sharing with him the value and the strength of using life insurance as a money tool. Years later, with hundreds of thousands of dollars in those policies and at a time when the automotive market was temporarily drying up; he used those policies to subsidize his business expenses. He was afraid he might get behind and wouldn't want the employees to hear about that since he might then lose them, and they were the key to his prosperity.

I had heard stories over the years of famous people who used their cash values to keep going. Some of these stories totally grabbed my attention. Hopefully, they will interest you.

The first name I saw was **Walt Disney**. When he was trying to raise capital in 1953 to help fund the building of Disneyland, he couldn't get the banks to lend him the money he needed. Mr. Disney decided to use money from his cash value life insurance and began building on the land we know today as Disneyland in California. The banks seeing his commitment, quickly jumped in and gave him the financial support he needed.

Another name that caught my eye was that of **J.C. Penney**. When the Great Depression hit, Mr. Penney owned a department store that like all the others around him, became cash starved. He needed money to pay his employees. He turned to his life insurance policy and it provided funds for the next few months to get him through the initial upheaval. Many of his competitors went out of business during this period, but he survived and as a result was one of only a few stores left. This survivor got all the business and Mr. Penney's success story is history.

I was a little surprised to see **Ray Kroc** mentioned. However, like most businessmen in a start-up position, he was strapped for the cash he needed to pay his key employees. Ray Kroc turned to his life insurance cash values for the money needed and was able to compensate those who were critical to his future success. He also used the cash values to begin his marketing campaign for his now famous, Ronald McDonald character.

One name making news with life insurance was Senator John McCain when he ran in 2007 as a presidential candidate. The senator needing a cash infusion went to the banks, but there was a not so unique requirement. John McCain had to take out an additional life insurance policy on himself with the bank as beneficiary. I guess the bank wanted to be sure they got their money back.

Even before acquiring any other loans, **Senator John McCain** secured initial campaign financing for his presidential bid by using his life insurance policy as collateral. Without knowing the specific details, the senator had his life insurance as a financial safety net. Turned out in his case, from the information I read, he needed both policies to be in place to satisfy creditor demands. Obviously, the death benefit in this instance was a key element in making loans.

Most business owners understand the need for liquidity, especially when banks tighten the screws making loans difficult to get. Larger businesses understand this, they appreciate the many uses of whole life insurance not merely for business succession planning, but more importantly in their day to day operation.

There is this foolish belief that permanent policy life insurance premiums are too high and the "cost" creates more stress on the daily need for capital.

Isn't it ironic, when business owners learn how to use the 'living' values of life insurance, they want all they can get?

They are in fact becoming their own finance company, their own bank. The savings in their businesses when using life insurance are huge.

I remember another situation where there were three shareholders in a closely held company that knew each other from their boyhood days. They went to the same schools and after only a few years out of college decided to go into business for themselves.

The first few years were a struggle, but they eventually began succeeding as they matured in their business. They were very close as friends and often they and their wives got together to either go to dinner or just hang out in one of their homes.

They had five employees and as business picked up, they wanted to help these five people prepare for retirement as well as they did for themselves. They installed a 401(k)-retirement plan and in the first two years, they managed to make contributions.

It was about this time when one of the three young owners developed a serious illness and shortly thereafter died. Unfortunately, they knew they needed life insurance to complete a buy-sell agreement, and they never considered key man coverage. They simply never got around to it. They thought permanent insurance was too expensive and they didn't want to waste their money on term. They also believed that at their young ages, none of them were going to die soon. After all, they were young and like most young men, they were immortal.

The young man who died was also their salesman and he was the one who built outside relationships for their business success. Their wives were all under the impression the business would continue and the one who was a widow would be able to cash out her husbands' share. Within a month of her husband's death, our widow showed up at the business to ask for her husband's share of the company, to which she was entitled.

She was told there was nothing in the business except a small amount of working capital and they weren't able to compensate her. When she showed up a few weeks later with her attorney, the story was repeated and she learned that there was an even direr situation developing for the company. Her husband's death left them with no one to replace the sales he brought in. Business revenues were dropping quickly following her husband's death.

They would soon be filing bankruptcy papers. Meanwhile, the employees they wanted to help with a retirement plan were being let go. She ended up with nothing from the business, the two surviving shareholders started another company with a different name doing the same kind of business, and they hired a salesperson to replace their deceased partner.

They started making money again and could see the light at the end of the tunnel, but the widow lost everything. She had nothing to show for her husband's loyalty and friendship for his two partners. The retirement plan assets she received had two years of contributions and earnings. That was all she received.

If instead of putting money into the retirement plan for themselves, they had purchased the right kind of life insurance, they would have received money to hold onto everything and find a sales person. The widow would have received her husband's fair share of the business.

Ironically, they would also have been building their own cash reserve going forward and that in itself would have saved them many tens of thousands of dollars going forward. The product with the incidental "death benefit" would have served multiple purposes and everyone would have come away in the best manner possible.

The company failure to put first things first, and protect itself from the death or disability of a key person was the very cause of it's failure.

The procedures remain the same businesses and individuals for creating your own financing 'type' of company. The main difference is that a business adds more zeros to the numbers.

A restaurant owner I know needed $135,000 for new equipment and tables. He has two sources for the funds. He has to choose between a bank and his life insurance. His goal was to pay back the source of funds over the following five years. The bank wanted 14% on any money lent to him for his business, and considering the bank's risk with restaurants, that seems a fair rate according to the owner's accountant. I helped him with the numbers using the two methods he had chosen.

Optional Financing through:

	The bank	Life Insurance A	Life Insurance B
Monthly Payment	$ 3,141	$ 2,548	$ 2,250
5-year Total Pyts	$ 188,472	$ 152,858	$ 135,000
Payments Saved		**$ 35,614**	**$ 53,472**
Cash Available	**$ - 0 -**	**$ 180,660**	**$ 159,400**

As you can see in Life Insurance A, the life insurance payments saved $35,614 over the bank. Additionally, the $135,000 in cash value continued to grow during the five years, just as if there were no loan against it. His cash value five years after the loan, and based on the loan amount had grown to $180,660. The restaurant owner paid $152,858 for a $135,000 policy loan. He then has another $45,660 added to his cash values. If he had used the bank, he is out $188,472. Now, that's a spread.

In the numbers under Life Insurance B, the owner uses dividends to cover the interest and pays only the net amount of the loan. Since dividends were used, the life insurance values grew to about $160,000. Not quite as good as in "A" above, but nonetheless, it is quite good.

The savings either way above in the insurance columns are quite a few hamburgers every month. Then too, there is the opportunity to use that money again which would not be true if he used a bank. If the owner had used savings, the immediate impact is that the savings are gone.

There are key points and rules to follow. While you have the flexibility with life insurance to make your own rules, these are a few rules to understand and work with in the illustration above.

a) When using loans on life insurance, the cash values are guaranteed to continue growing. When initiating the loan, the insurance company uses the cash value as collateral and issues a check simply on a client's request without asking for reasons why you want the money or checking your credit scores.

b) You should get your agent to give you the amount necessary to pay off the loan in the time period you choose. You should replenish your well.

c) You can always use the dividends in the participating life insurance policy to pay the interest due on the loan. The net result is you are making purchases with a zero-out of pocket-interest loan for as long a period as you want. Be sure to understand the consequences of any actions you are taking. Using the dividends reduces the overall growth rate of the policy.

d) You should consider paying the higher amount the lender wanted, but to yourself. Use the spread you saved to either pay off the loan quicker or Investing the Rest. In the illustration above, that would be about $7,100 a year. Investing the savings conservatively over 20 years and adding them to the cash values would bring this total to a hefty figure. Remember, that's your money. Seems a bit better than ending up with zero in the bank.

Two ideas that can be of help. If at the time of purchase, the finance company offers you a zero-interest rate for a specified period, take it. If it is a substantial amount of money and you can't meet the terms, you can then use the cash values in your life insurance to rescue you and pay off any outstanding balance before any financing expenses kick in. Saves your credit score as well.

Life insurance loans aren't seen by anyone but you and the insurance company. They are private loans. The insurance company will never call or notify you if you fail to make payment unless you put the policy itself in trouble.

How would you have financed it? Remember, the life insurance cash value continues to grow and the values are guaranteed to grow. This

process can be repeated over and over again. Is it meaningful for you?
You do the math.

Chapter 7

Other Concepts

> **"Good advice is almost certain to be ignored,
> but that's no reason not to give it."**
> Agatha Christie

It's likely that anyone over the age of 25 has experienced the use of other peoples' money. By that point it may have been that they borrowed from mom and dad, cars were financed, credit cards applied for and used, as well as direct bank loans executed. They have learned or should have, that no matter who leant them money, the lender expects to be paid back.

In this first scenario, as an agent, I have heard all the arguments over life insurance when young families are starting out. They are told by their 'expert' friends and relatives that they should buy term and invest the rest. Put all they can into their retirement plan at work, and halfheartedly to keep an emergency fund in the bank. I have seen people take money from their savings and other accounts and some borrow directly from their 401(k) or the bank.

The reasons are numerous, but people, especially young people, often feel they need something right away and lack the funds to do whatever it is they need or want at that moment. A few people, comparatively speaking, have needs that are true financial emergencies.

On the other hand, there are people buying things they don't need, with money they don't have, to impress people that don't matter.

I don't watch or listen to their shows, but going on YouTube, you can watch as those famous Guru's, Suze Orman and Dave Ramsey say that, "you should only buy level term insurance." They say that, "permanent policies like whole life insurance are bad investments."

If one's policies are static, that is, never used, then these two gurus could be right. Life insurance is a bad investment. HOWEVER, I am sorry you two gurus' even foster that belief, because that isn't the true story. Whole Life Insurance shouldn't sit on idle.

Again, there is a good reason that for nearly two centuries the words Whole Life means just that. It is for one's Whole Life, the death benefit actually becomes incidental as it should be, until of course it is needed at one's death.

It's tragically a mistake that entertainers like the two mentioned above, don't' take the time to dive into their subject matter and understand the insurance product they are attacking. They might learn how to benefit from it, and then help people by educating them as to the many living uses of guaranteed whole life insurance.

Too many entertainers do not make their money by being supportive of events, items and other people. They make their 'fortunes' by attacking, by standing out and the consequences don't matter. You see, it doesn't fit their agenda. Unfortunately, accepting these self-proclaimed 'experts,' people are listening to them and reacting, and that is a pity.

Whole Life Insurance is Good News
When you Use it!

BUY TERM AND INVEST THE REST

Stating this once more, over the past fifty years when helping people purchase life insurance, I came to anticipate hearing those famous words from those who accept the fact that they need life insurance, "I've been told I should buy term and invest the rest."

That expression is usually coming from people who know nothing more than the person they are sharing their wisdom with. It's now a common expression, imbedded in our think tanks over many decades for those who look at life insurance as an expense. Too many insurance agents with different goals easily agree with them, just to make the sale. Unfortunately, too often neither the buyer nor the seller recognizes that they have it backwards.

The honest response is that term policies are marketed with full knowledge of the life insurance companies, that only 1.2% will ever end up in a death benefit. A recurring study started by Dr. Williams at Penn State University came up with that number many decades ago. In fact, very few term policies go full term. That is, to the end of the coverage period. Many are lapsed along the way when people become tired of throwing their money away.

I'll never forget a conversation I had with an actuary who worked the numbers for a life insurance company. If he designed a package where the mortality rate would be beyond one and a half percent, he would be fired. True, I heard that a few years back, but other actuaries I have spoken with since, have confirmed they too felt that way.

I, as just one salesperson among hundreds of thousands in this industry, cannot begin to tell you how many older people I've heard say, "I wasted all that money on a term policy." I've heard that exasperation at least once a month on average for roughly fifty years. It's hard hearing those words from a person who not too long afterwards learned that they have become uninsurable.

A friend who recently retired came into my office. He was upset with me. Actually, he was angry. He told me I should have been more forceful with him and 'made' him buy permanent life insurance. Now that his wife might need those dollars, they aren't there. He saved regularly and with a decent percent of his income in his company's 401(k). Suddenly, looking at his account, it wasn't any pot of gold. Then he told me his doctor gave him a short-term outlook.

The reality today is that most people acquiring life insurance feel they are "budgeting" for the premiums. It is not thought of as a high priority, rather they view it as a necessary expense. They in fact, want that low premium, and then they can forget about it. When they hear the words 'life insurance,' their only thoughts are that it is something for when they die. You know, way out there, somewhere lost in the future. They are too busy 'not listening,' and eventually the sad result is the loss of tens of thousands of dollars.

Coming from Philadelphia, I know too many people around here will spend more time watching just one professional game on television, than they will devote during a year's time, to learning what they might be better doing with their money. The sad thing again is, we are not talking about just a few bucks.

Sometimes being repetitive is important. A former Pennsylvania Insurance Commissioner, Harry Gross many years ago stated, "Two people will buy the same amount of life insurance from two different companies. They will pay the same amount for twenty years and one will have twice as much money accumulated as the other in a policy,

AND NEITHER ONE WILL EVER KNOW IT."

People would rather talk about their 'glitzy' investments than life insurance. Try going to a party, announce when asked what you do, say you sell life insurance, and observe what happens next. You will know you have been abruptly ostracized when you feel like you are suddenly alone in the artic.

A well-known sports journalist, author, and television personality in Philadelphia, Ray Didinger was doing a radio show when he shared this story.

> *He was taking his seat on an airplane and a man reading the sports pages from a local newspaper was sitting next to him. Ray knew from watching the man go through the newspaper that this man was a sports' fan.*

> *Ray also knew from his many experiences that if this man knew who he was, he would be in a non-stop conversation for the next four hours. Greeting one another, this man seemed to be very talkative and told Ray what he did for a living. He naturally proceeded to ask Ray what he did and Ray quickly said, "I sell insurance."*

> *Ray reported that was the quietest four-hour airplane ride he has ever had. The man didn't say another*

word. Ray being what seems to be a very humble man, looking back to this moment, was sorry he misled this man. It's not something he typically does.

Unfortunately, this other passenger provided one reason why so few know the real, the living benefits of life insurance. No one wants to listen. When it comes to life insurance, people cannot get away from the notion that they pay money for a death benefit that <u>won't happen in their lifetime</u> that is for decades in the future.

If they only realized how important life insurance is to their day to day living, it could make a significant difference. However, they can't see it as anything but an item in their 'spending' budget.

Upon hearing those words from Harry Gross all those years ago, I like many other knowledgeable agents knew instantly the truth in what he said. There's that lack of attention to what people are doing. Go ahead, buy a car, spend days looking and at the end of the day, they wind up saving a few hundred dollars-maybe. Yet their life insurance policies could be making them hundreds of thousands of dollars during their working years and even in retirement, **AND THEY WILL NEVER KNOW IT**. Yes, once again, I said, hundreds of thousands of dollars.

Yet, when purchasing what could be the most important product during their lifetime, and for their loved ones, they don't give it the "time of day." Amazing! That fact however, weighs very little with people that are 'budgeting' for life insurance. All they care about is what has the lowest impact on their budget. The problem again with that thought, the **best** impact on their budget isn't the term insurance.

It is a life insurance industry problem when insurance agents use the same standard proposals to support their respective positions. Both sides, permanent life and term insurance illustrations highlight their positions. The 'term' guy shows 'cheap' term and invests the rest as if anyone would really do that.

It is an unfortunate position not to understand that term insurance is 'temporary' coverage and should the insured become highly rated during that term coverage period, or forget to pay a term insurance premium, well, good luck. There is no parachute. When those term premiums the insured paid are added up, most are simply thinking to themselves, 'ok, it's lost money.'

Now, for some more hard figures. In this simplistic example, the person who purchases permanent whole life insurance saves $10,000 in what would have been additional payments to credit card companies, doing it over and over again at four-year intervals and investing the difference. Do the math! Take a look at what that person has achieved at 5% returns over the years. Now, this is investing the 'right' difference and does not include the life insurance cash values which continually grow.

End of Year	Investment Account Value
10	$ 25,647
20	$ 80,553
30	$ 156,859
40	$ 283,783

When added to one's cash values, this makes for very attractive returns.

I know for a fact, that our entertainment gurus never explored this utilization of life insurance policies or they never would have commented in such an ugly way. There would have been no excuse for it. As it is, they've shown their lack of depth in understanding whatever it is they disagree with. Their calculators never take into account the 'using' of life insurance cash values. If they had, our two "entertainers" would never have misled their audience, at least, I hope not.

Some people really believe they won't need insurance later in life because their investments will solve that problem. Good luck with that when the markets tumble and you start sucking air, while removing principal from your accounts. Watch the negative effects on those dollars. Be the surviving spouse in that too frequent scenario.

> One of the best reasons I've seen for life insurance in later years, and it is only one of the reasons, is to use it to pay the income taxes due on qualified 'inherited' accounts. A husband and wife have a half million dollars in an IRA. At the second death, the money goes to their children who pay the income taxes due on that money. It could be $150,000

> Take $5,000 to pay a premium on second to die whole life. After ten years, there would be no premiums due. The $5,000 buys $200,000 of second to die joint life insurance that your children would have to reimburse them for the taxes.

Think of it, pay just one percent of the account for ten years or so, and the taxes are covered. That's a total of ten percent spread out over ten years and it can cover one hundred percent of the taxes due.

Additionally, the cash value in these policies could be used over and over again by the husband and wife who are purchasing the life insurance. They haven't given their money away, and yet, they are able to protect the money they worked so hard to accumulate.

That being said, the real mistake is how insurance agents use proposals to support their position. Both term and permanent illustrations will use similar proposals with the main difference being the rate of interest required to equal or beat the other.

However, that's not the end of the story. You see, the numbers inside the cash value life insurance are static, not used. If the cash values are used, the results can easily double the illustrative numbers. Before we get there, this is a sample comparison I've seen over the many years I've been in this business.

Male, age 45, non-smoker, $250,000 of Death Benefit, Preferred Risk. Premiums are paid for 20 years in both contracts, term coverage ends, permanent continues.

Year	Term Premium	Permanent Premium	Difference at 5% net	Permanent Cash Value
1	$445	$4,780	$4,552	$ -0-
5	$445	$4,780	$25,152	$14,400
10	$445	$4,780	$57,252	$43,625
20	$445	$4,780	$150,509	$124,615

Yes, this comparison is typical, but it is WRONG!

Doing it this way and in the early years, term easily defeats the permanent insurance and the permanent eventually catches up in values. At age 65, the insurance amount in term is zero while the permanent has a death benefit of $342,000 and growing while going forward. The 5% rate of return on the above side investment for term is after-tax. The values in the permanent insurance will continue to grow, even though premiums stopped in the 20ᵗʰ year.

Now, depending on which viewpoint is being pushed, I can adjust the returns accordingly to make my side win. Thus, if I'm selling term, I would increase the interest after-tax returns. On the permanent side of the ledger, I might reduce the interest rate for the outside investments to a lower after-tax return and could have made a strong argument for that position. While both views can be properly proposed, as I said a moment ago, this is not the end of the story.

Remember that we can use cash values to finance our larger purchases and save quite a bit over the regular interest payments on those financed charges every month. Let's recall those numbers I used for showing this on the previous page and the 'savings invested at 5% for both sides. With comparable outlays, whole life vs term and investing the rest, and investing the savings on interest in financed purchases as shown a page earlier.

The term and invest the rest concept against whole life and using it as shown earlier would result after 20 years with:

Term Insurance with difference at net 5%	$150,509
The Whole Life Total Cash Values	$124,615
The Whole Life Used from above would return	$205,168

Oh, do I love this! Notice that at net 5% return every year on one's ability to save or invest, the difference isn't even close. In this example, I used a low amount for finance rewards. When USING my life insurance cash values, the life insurance blows the Term and Invest the Rest concept right out the window. The difference of a plus 36% over the term is quite noticeable.

It's not even close. If the investment returns were higher, the larger the advantage for whole life insurance. The more the life insurance is used to save interest on financing, the larger the advantage for whole life insurance.

After twenty years the term policy most usually 'terminates' while the whole life, while using dividends, continues to grow without premiums being paid. The smarter person is using those cash values throughout life, and the life insurance death benefit which also continues growing passes on to the spouse or the next generation. Recalling that frequently heard expression,

The rich get richer
While the poor get poorer!

Let's shake it up! Remember, "Ideas are a dime a dozen, but the person who puts them into practice is priceless."

The smarter get rich
They have a tool to use
The uninformed get poorer!

Want to take a guess at which method is the more effective method of building wealth? Who would have thought Whole Life Insurance? Does this make a difference? You bet it does!

If nothing else, as demonstrated, this puts the 'term and invest the rest' theory to bed. Even if a person were disciplined enough to continue investing the rest and keep paying the term premiums, it just doesn't work the way it is supposed to produce results. If you do a lot of financing, and we all do, this program will explode the term and invest the rest concept as a myth. Remember and yes again, as others have stated over the years,

We finance everything we buy, cash or credit.

Before going further, I will admit there are a limited number of short term situations where purchasing term life insurance does work, but not the theory of 'buy term and invest the rest.' It never works over the long run for the benefit of any party to a life insurance policy.

IN A 401(k) RETIREMENT PLAN

The odds are that most of those reading these pages cannot remember when the 401(k) became the retirement plan of choice or what were the reasons. Until the early 80's (yes, from the last century), pensions and profit-sharing plans were by far and away, the primary source of retirement funds for most people.

Once brought to the surface as a viable retirement plan, most employers began focusing their sights on this part of the IRS codes for retirement plans. However, their reasons for doing this weren't necessarily in the best interest of the employee.

Until this time, pensions and profit-sharing plans were considered expensive. An employer would typically set aside in addition to the employee's salary, three to fifteen percent of an employee's earnings for the pension or profit-sharing plan.

When the 401(k) came into existence, many employers loved it. This plan was funded by the employees themselves, with a small match from the employer. This put those dollars employers were using for employees back into the employer's hands.

Never were any plans designed to put wealth into the equation. They were designed to help Employees Bridge the gap from their working years to produce a stream of income in addition to their social security checks and other assets the employees may have.

Today, employees may mistakenly view their retirement accounts as a 'savings' account. It is NOT a savings account, it is future income. It should not be used for emergencies or opportunities that come along. Yet, unfortunately for too many people, it is the only money they have set aside.

The so-called effects of a recent 'government shut-down' on employees temporarily out of work was meant to draw sympathy for workers. For me, it was an indictment of our 'middle class' citizens. All of us throughout our lives have heard the expression, "Save money for a rainy day."

Yet, here there are stories on television news of employees losing their homes to forfeitures by missing one week's pay. Really, whose fault is that. These workers have long-term security. Something isn't right, and it's not the shut-down. Unless of course, the worker wasn't putting anything aside for occurrences such as these. These employees needed hand-outs after only three weeks. What am I missing? No, what are they missing?

The media eats this stuff up. "If it bleeds, it leads." If it doesn't bleed, the media knows how to do make it.

We all need to set money aside and a retirement plan is not the place to put our money to be withdrawn for next weeks' food. Once money is borrowed from an employer's retirement plan, you must pay it back, but you have lost those values forever. When employees pay back a loan, they usually forego contributing to the plan. They use what would have been contributions to pay back the loan. The money withdrawn plus any potential earnings on that money is gone forever.

If your plan at work allows for life insurance, that adds a slightly different dimension to this picture. By using the 401(k) to purchase permanent guaranteed participating life insurance, we can see a difference. Just check out some of these benefits.

a) You are using tax-deductions for your purchase. *
b) If you are in a 20% tax bracket, you save 36% on the premium. The government is subsidizing the premium. Considering that everything you buy outside of a qualified retirement plan is after-tax, this enters into the equation.
c) **It is the only asset in the retirement plan that's guaranteed to keep growing when you borrow from it.** **
d) There is a required pay back on 401(k) loans, not to exceed 5 years and includes interest under the federal regulations. Your money in the policy just keeps growing.
e) Dividends can be applied to premiums inside your retirement plan allowing for money you are contributing to the plan to go to other investments.
f) Life insurance can be viewed as all or part of your 'safe' investment inside your portfolio of investments. In the 401(k),

- Life insurance is deductible, however there is a current economic benefit applied to the death benefit. You will be given a 1099 for a very small dollar amount that is reportable. As a current economic benefit, the pure death portion of the policy is taxed. For instance, I just saw one premium of $7,510 that is deductible, but has a reportable amount of $125 and the tax on that in a 20% tax bracket is $25.

- The premiums for life insurance should be in addition to your contributions to the retirement plan. The difference is the taxes saved by using the plan for premiums.

- Earlier I said that the death benefit that is the life insurance is actually 'incidental' to the life insurance policy. The IRS allows the insurance inside a business qualified plan and calls the life insurance 'incidental' in the plan.

- **At the time of separation for a participant from the plan, the life insurance cannot be rolled over and taxes are due on what is considered 'constructive receipt' of a plan's assets. Having dividends inside the cash values helps you and in many cases the dividends will cover any and all taxes due on a rollout. The policy will lose a corresponding amount, but it will continue to grow tax-deferred and provide all the benefits of a privately-owned contract, which it now is.

At the time of purchase, if you want to use the life insurance immediately for financing you can. In addition to the required premium, roll over some of your other assets inside the 401(k) into the policy. You are limited to how much, usually not more than the actual premium itself. You could start using the cash values almost immediately. Each insurance company has its own rules for this and it should be compliant with the law. The agent can be a very useful asset helping you with this.

While the life insurance death benefit cannot be rolled out of a 401(k) into an IRA, it can be rolled over into another companies' 401(k) if allowed by documentation in the new plan. Thus, giving you the option of 'buying' it out perhaps using dividends, or rolling it over into another 401(k). Another option is to surrender the policy and the cash values become assets in your plan account. Personally, this is the least favorable option.

The 401(k) plan makes an excellent vehicle for your permanent life insurance. In fact, for many people that have this availability it makes great sense. The real advantages of a 401(k) are the 'phantom' contributions going into the plan and an employer match when available. Employees don't miss what they don't see in their paychecks. In this case, we have money doing double duty.

The arguments are strong not to use your retirement plan as a banking instrument, because you lose the potential for opportunity growth and have to pay the interest on your money. Life insurance cash values inside the plan however, keep growing when used and once more, the interest can be directed to other investments. It doesn't get any better than this.

The argument for not borrowing from your 401(k) has lost it's merit when the 'fixed' asset you borrow from continues to grow, regardless of the loan.

Chapter 8

CHANGING YOUR WORLD

> **"Change your thoughts
> And you change your world."**
> *Norman Vincent Peale*

You know we really aren't all that different. Race, ideology, nationality, we share the same feelings, ideas, concerns, and many other factors that make us one. For instance, one common desire we share is to pass our savings on to our children and grandchildren, it's nearly a universal feeling.

A high percentage of retirees put money into Certificates of Deposit, savings accounts, and money market accounts. It's not the account we want, it's the safety these accounts provide for us. This is money we may need for a family emergency or maybe a vacation, but until that time, we want our money to be secure and liquid.

Frequent investment advertisements say they know how to make your money work harder so you don't. I have always found that to be a poor description of money invested. I prefer language that is different in both scope and meaning.

The advertisements say,
**"Make your money work harder,
So you don't have to."**

I say again,
**"Make your money work smarter
And you won't have to."**

We may want to donate some of what we have to charity, but then we would be taking something away from our children. We may want a higher return on our investments, but that comes with additional risks. We have wants, but we know that fulfilling these wants leaves us with less cash for tomorrow.

The older one is, the more we look to enjoying every day of a shortened future. We envision all the good times ahead and then that money concern enters into the picture, but it doesn't stop us.

I have been filling these pages with all the values found in a life insurance contract, the right kind that is. Now, I would like to demonstrate how life insurance can remove so many of these concerns and add additional benefits.

You will also see the opportunity for those who consider themselves too old for this or are perhaps 'highly rated' or uninsurable. The solutions with these concepts are seemingly unlimited.

There is one business method for using life insurance that has just as many, if not more related applications for families. It is a concept that has been around longer than my fifty years in the business. I hope you will find this knowledge to be as useful for you as it has been for so many others.

SPLIT DOLLAR

What a distinguishing concept! When we learn and understand that there are different parties to a life insurance policy, we can begin to conceive of the many unique ways available to structure the policy. Earlier there was an example of Split-Dollar for businesses, yet there are many applications for using this procedure.

While many insurance agents never think of the individual outside the world of business, it has many uses for the family. Some might contend that this is a complex issue, but in reality, it is simple. Once the set-up is done, there is little else to be concerned with.

We start with the knowledge that there are four parties to a life insurance contract. There is an insured, an owner, a payor, and a beneficiary. You can have as little as two parties involved, such as the insured and the beneficiary. One of which can assume the role of the other parties as an owner or payer.

The fun part is watching how we make these parts come together to fulfill so many needs and wants. I hope when we finish this chapter, you are saying, "Who would've thought?"

The insured is the one with the 'exposure' to life and death. Fairly obvious! The owner, who is generally the payer, owns the rights to the contract. The owner can change beneficiaries, use the cash values in the contract, and change those options in the contract that are allowed to be changed.

The payer is the individual who writes the checks to the insurance company. It can be anyone of the four parties having rights in the policy. I'd better state again, you are writing those checks to yourself, and in the best way possible. The money goes from one account into another with the owner's name on the account. You are switching your money from one pocket to another pocket, but they are both your pockets.

There can be one or more primary beneficiaries and also one or more secondary beneficiaries. This is the person(s) or entities receiving the proceeds from the policy at the 'insured's' death.

Again, the cash values and dividends are controlled by the owner. Owners can use these dollars, in any way they want. Better yet, unless the owner signs paperwork to put a lien on these cash values, they are creditor proof in most states.

Our First Situation, Too Old or Uninsurable

Ok, now that we have a basic understanding of the parties in a life insurance contract, we can begin to tackle problems associated in using life insurance as a funding tool. I am going to use myself as the old guy or if you like, you can think of me as uninsurable. Sadly, I really do qualify for both of these descriptions.

Ok, I just learned that at my age I am not a good candidate for life insurance, but I want to use life insurance to create my own savings account and to finance my larger purchases. Why should I not be able to help myself this way to finance vacations, buy a car, or fix my roof.

The agent has explained how I can use life insurance for financing purposes as early as the first year if I so desire, then after some discussion on my age and my health, explains that it would be useless for me to apply. Great! I can get insurance on my car, my refrigerator, my television, and my home, but I'm beyond that. Ugh! My appliances have a brighter future than me. And I was looking forward to my next thirty years; so much for that.

However, my agent's a sharp guy and he has an idea. He wants to show me how I can accomplish my goals. To be able to save on finance charges and pass more on to my heirs than might otherwise be possible with 'safe' accounts. He reminds me that the insurance in this program should be considered incidental. That works out to be very important.

My primary goal is to achieve better financial goals than I would otherwise have in my bank accounts. Remember, I want my money working smarter, not harder. Further, I want my children to inherit my savings. I don't want to squander efforts to strengthen my cash reserves.

The agent explains that from our discussion, that I told him my children are healthy. He goes on to explain that I could purchase the life insurance, not on myself, but on one or more of them.

He some key points for doing this,

a) I would be the payer of premiums, and it would be my responsibility to make the necessary payments.

b) I would be the owner of the policy and would have access to the cash values.

c) One of them would be the insured. It would work with a daughter, a son-in-law etc. In this example, I will use a son.

d) The beneficiary would be split. Because, if my son were to predecease me, I wouldn't want the money I have put into this account to be lost, and I would want the beneficiary he chose getting the greater amount of death benefit.

e) So, if my son predeceased me, which I don't want to think about, my payments into the life insurance would come back to me in full, loan or no loan, plus an interest rate of my choosing. The beneficiary form would say I was getting all payments for premiums back plus, at an annual rate of return of 3%, maybe 5%. The choice is mine. The balance, the pure death benefit – the amount between what I get and the total death benefit – going to his direct heirs. I would have my money back plus interest and his loved ones would have their fair share.

f) Should I die before my son, which is to be expected, I can name the successor owner to the policy. For Instance, I could have my son become the owner of the contract as if he were the payer and owner all along. He would get the cash reserves, the life insurance, and all rights therein.

The result with my 'savings' is that I would have the use of those dollars for covering any financing on purchases I make. The money is there for me to use, and again, if unfortunately, something did happen to my son, I would recover all my premiums plus interest.

Once again, there is more to the death proceeds. While I would recover payments plus interest, he has the option to name whomever he wants to get the 'pure insurance' on the contract.

Let's say that the face amount of the contract was $250,000 and I put in $4,000 a year for 10 years. During this time too, dividends purchased another $25,000 of life insurance and the total death benefit is $275,000. On the beneficiary form, I elected to receive as my portion of the death benefit, all my premiums at 4%. At this point my son dies.

a) I would have deposited $40,000 over the ten years.

b) My deposits at 4% total $49,945 and the insurance company would send me a check for that amount. That would be true even if there were a loan on the policy.

c) The net death benefit that is the 'pure insurance,' the amount between the cash values (at interest) and the total death amount would go to his beneficiary. In this example, the difference is the current death benefit of $275,000 and $49,975.

d) I would have my $49,975 and his beneficiary would receive $225,025, less any outstanding loans.

e) Removing the loan at death is possible using what is called, "a fifth dividend option." In this case, it allows for the death benefit selected plus the cash values, plus any dividend additions. After all is said and done, my son's beneficiary would receive not the $225,025, but $297,000(EST.). The loan is more than made up for. (Life insurance death benefit, $275,000 plus $42,000 less a loan of $20,000.)

His beneficiary would have received a death benefit and my son never made any payments. His family would have protection and I would have my payments and an annual interest for making the payments. Protection was provided for everyone.

That is not the end of the story. Again, as indicated above, I as the owner in the contract can name succession ownership, and if I so elect, irrevocably. If my spouse is alive, I could name her and then at her death, my son as the next beneficiary or make my son, should my spouse pass before me, my successor owner.

My son would have inherited all the rights and the cash values in the policy and his heirs would receive the full death benefit when he dies. Perhaps I'm not comfortable with that thought. Maybe my son's widow's next husband is someone I don't know or may not like, I have even more options.

I could make the beneficiary a trust and direct how those proceeds are to be used for her and my grandchildren. There could be provisions to my liking should she remarry. As the owner of the policy, the options belong to me.

In another scenario, maybe it's better to make a son-in-law the insured and my daughter the successor owner. She could keep the insurance on him, even in the worst of events, such as they might divorce at some point. Now, that's a thought!

In any event, the owner of the contract has the rights to the cash values and can use these dollars no matter who the insured may be. At this point, I would want my son or daughter to consult a full-time estate planning attorney. Leaving money to loved ones should be a situation where all the methods are considered, even a spendthrift type clause in a trust might be useful.

I would endorse the 'SPLIT DOLLAR' methodology for all those having insurability problems. Those who have a savings account, want to make a better rate of return on their money using it for financing, helping their children and grandchildren and want to protect their savings, I know of no better way.

Think about it, how can you justify keeping money set aside for emergencies or other long-term purposes, in a saving account, Certificate of Deposit or Money Market account? Unless for some clueless purpose, you just like having it there.

Your money can be doing so much more.

EQUILIZING INHERITANCES

There was one client with three children. He was proud of his farm and wanted to keep it in the family after he was gone. The farm was worth nearly $3 million. He was particularly happy that one of his children, a daughter wanted to be a vet. She lived on the farm with her parents and proved to be extremely helpful with the cows on his farm. Her two brothers meanwhile, pursued other careers.

After many years he decided to sit down and review how he would divide his legacy. He had delayed doing this because he didn't want his farm sold, but there were three children and this was a problem. The farm would only support one family, and only one was needed to take care of the farm.

His daughter wanted it, but how could he give her a $3 million farm and not the others. When we sat down, knowing his problem, I told him I had a solution.

He could use some of his farm's cash reserve and purchase a $2 million whole life policy making his two sons the beneficiaries and leave the farm to his daughter. Since the sons would have inherited about $1 million each had the farm been sold to be split three ways, the farmer was happy. Surprisingly, the sons were fine with this idea even though their sister would get the $3 million farm.

The insurance from his viewpoint would be a financial burden. He would have to sell something off just to pay one year's premium. We discussed this in depth. He did keep a large cash reserve, but that was needed for emergencies or any opportunities that came along. Running a farm was not without its financial ups and downs.

At this point, I shared with him how he could transfer over a ten year period or so, the annual premiums from his cash reserve. He liked the fact that this new account was liquid and even more so that roughly ninety percent of his first-year premium was available to him if he needed it. By the fifth year, one hundred percent of all his premiums were available.

While the new policy would provide safety and liquidity with his money, he looked at the life insurance as yes, incidental. However, he knew the life insurance would be important to those he loved in the not too distant future.

The farmer's attorney when drafting the necessary documents, added a feature so there would not be any animosity later if she sold the farm. She would have to split some of the proceeds proportionately with her brothers if she sold within five years of inheriting the farm. They were all agreeable.

The farmer was delighted too, he had discovered a new way, a less expensive way, a profitable way, to get funding for projects he had from time to time. It was so easy when he thought about it. Just moving money from one account to another. He came away knowing that not only his children were getting what was rightfully theirs, but he was making a profit with this new way of financing.

CHARITY WITH SPLIT-DOLLAR

I can't tell you the number of times an insurance agent will hear during their careers that a client would like to leave money to their favorite charity. The problem confronting nearly all of them is that, regardless of financial situations, they don't want to short-change their children's inheritance. The charity would frequently be put aside.

Remember, these are the folks who put money into 'safe' accounts to make sure they had it for an emergency and to either help or leave it for their children. A common scenario!

Split-Dollar can be a great feature for many people. Whenever I discuss planning for the distribution of one's estate, which may be very small or large, I ask if they would like to leave anything to charity. Invariably, they wish they could leave more to their children.

When we do our discovery process (fact finding) with a client, we regularly come across cash. It may be in the form of a Certificate of Deposit, money market account held at a bank, cash in a brokerage account. Another place we have come across cash equivalents from time to time, and yes these are still around, savings bonds purchased decades earlier, which may or may not be earning interest. It has been no surprise to find more than a $100,000 in these older $25 and higher priced bonds.

People made an effort over the years to save this money, of course they don't want to lose it. Most often, the charity loses.

I met a lady in her sixties at a church function. She approached me after she was told by someone else that I sold life insurance. She had a personal question. She had $50,000 in a Certificate of Deposit that was maturing and a bank advisor wanted her to use it to purchase a Single Premium Life Insurance Policy. She could use the additional death proceeds as a donation to her church. We set up a meeting in my office for the next day and we threw some numbers around.

She was told how the values would grow at a nice rate of return and her beneficiary would receive the full death benefit at the time of her death. The $50,000 would purchase an insurance policy with a death benefit of around $110,000.

Going by what she remembered, she was not told that should she use the cash values, taxes would be applied to any gains in the policy. These contracts are considered taxable entities from day one and any earnings over the cash value are taxable when removed. Any dollars used above the cost basis, whether withdrawals or loans, are considered taxable. The basis (that is the amount she paid), would not be taxable. For me, that is never a good idea.

I asked her why she had the Certificate of Deposit, and she responded that it was set aside for an emergency, especially if one of her children needed it. This was the main reason for the account and she was hoping that she could also leave the Church a donation from this account. She said that's what gave the bank salesperson the idea of a single premium life insurance policy. She could leave the Church a fixed amount like $20,000 and the balance would go to her children.

I asked her if she really wanted to give up the flexibility of using those dollars. Once she understood my question, she said that she would prefer the money be available in case she did need it, and without the taxation. She didn't want the government getting any part of this money if that could be avoided.

When we got together, I showed her how she could spread the transfer of her funds over a ten-year period into a "twenty-year" pay life insurance policy. I explained how she could then apply dividends saved in the contract, plus future dividends to pay premiums. While dividends aren't guaranteed, the insurance company had never in all its more than 160 years failed to pay a dividend. By the way, while that statistic is very comforting to a client, it is equally as comfortable to me as an agent as well.

132

The cash values of the policy are hers. Hers to use as she wants, just like a bank account, one without having checks. No FDIC, but with the insurance company and the State Insurance Association which would, in my state, protect her up to $300,000 of her cash values.

The face amount of the insurance was for $150,000 (I like round numbers). Dividends would add to that figure starting after the second anniversary of the policy being in force.

I explained how she could divide the monies between her family and the church. She was delighted. She did however, manage to surprise me.

She decided to leave the cash values in the policy to her children, PLUS they were to get half of the life insurance proceeds above that amount and her church would receive the other half.

In one swift move, she would be passing on her savings to her children. Her heirs would be well ahead of what she originally had planned.

She was also giving the church about $50,000 at her death. She was delighted with that thought as well. This was something she had buried in her heart and now she could do it.

She also learned and now knows, that the cash values are there for her to use. She can and probably will use them to save on any future financing type expenses she may have. This lady is hitting a home run.

THE CHARITABLE REMAINDER TRUST (CRT)

This is for only a few, but is an extremely valuable tool. The appreciation of stocks and especially commercial property which includes rental properties, that has been depreciated and held for a long period of time can have serious tax consequences at the time of sale. Taxes for the Recapture of depreciation and capital gains can more than take its toll.

It is not an uncommon scene to see a $2 million property being sold and the seller owing the government through Capital Gain Taxes and Recapture of Depreciation, as much as $600,000 on the sale. Before that revelation, the seller was counting on the sale to earn $100,000 each year with the money invested at 5%. It's now 5% on $1.4 million. When the seller dies, the seller's children will pay state inheritance taxes with even less left over from the $1.4 million they inherited.

One of two well-known solutions to capital gains tax in this situation is to donate the property in trust to your favorite charity, all $2 million of it. The property is sold and the $2 million goes to the trust. The trust yields 5% per year, or $100,000 every year to the donors. There are also taxes to be saved potentially over the next five years, perhaps covering the entire income you receive from the trust.

The problem with that solution is that unless the trust is stated in some other, carefully scripted manner, the heirs will not receive any inheritance from these funds. There is a solution that benefits the seller, children, and a favorite charity.

Purchase a life insurance policy (such as survivor whole life), perhaps from income tax savings, and when the seller and spouse both die, the children will receive within week's $2 million income tax free. They should speak with their accountant and/or attorney and if the idea works, then carefully follow the road they give.

The winners in this scenario can be the family, the favorite charity, and the seller. Let's total this up and assume the seller and spouse live for only 7 years. They would have received in income $700,000. Their favorite charity gets $2 million and their family gets $2 million dollars. That's nearly $5 million out of property that would have yielded only $1.4 million. Not a bad haul and everybody wins.

WHAT A WEAPON FOR A BUSINESS, A FAMILY

It's like having 'money on steroids.'

Earlier I discussed business owners and the Split-Dollar concept. These business owners are the last warriors, the last of the real risk takers. These are our entrepreneurs, the business owners. This is especially true for those just starting out with a new or relatively new venture. In our changing society, it takes a person with a strong backbone to say, "I'm starting a new business."

The reason I am bringing this up again, is because a family is like a business. The wedding day creates an institution resembling the day a business opens its doors to the public. The owners are the key figures as are the breadwinners in a family.

A business owner's family frequently ask a question, what happens to us if you die? We don't know what to do with the business.

Likewise, the spouse of a breadwinner wants to know what happens to the family when death raises its head. How is the family to go on, what happens to their dreams? What happens for the children's education? How is the surviving spouse changing views on retirement? So many questions, so much doubt.

Business owners aren't out looking for someone else to offer them a job, they are not complaining to a television reporter, rather they are too busy trying to create jobs. We need more people like them.

If it's not the most important item on a business owners list of things needed, it's at least a close second, the need for a cash reserve. It might be there from the beginning of the business, but most often, it is built up over time.

Neither a business owner nor a breadwinner is ever quite sure when the sudden need for cash will arise. However, there is no doubt that this need will raise its head.

Here again, we see how a business owner is much like the head of a family, the main breadwinner. The financial replacements needed for a family when a breadwinner dies are magnified in the moment.

Whether you own a business or find yourself at the head of the family table, the many uses of guaranteed participating whole life insurance are invaluable to you while you are alive, and maybe invaluable to your heirs when you die.

Don't worry though, use the life insurance while you are alive.

USING A PROFESSIONAL LIFE INSURANCE REPRESENTATIVE

Being one of the longest active licensed insurance agents in the states of Pennsylvania and New Jersey, you can say I've seen a thing or two. One day just to check on my status, I called the insurance department. The young man at the other end of the phone pulled up my data. The next thing I heard is, "Holy s...., you're as old as dirt." Can't say I totally appreciated that, but I understood. Add to that, I have been licensed in the world of securities going back to about 1981.

I have watched as many Investment Advisors sold life insurance and many Life Insurance agents sold investments. I can tell you it takes more creativity to market the life insurance because to many Investment Advisors, the required depth of life insurance understanding, takes them deeper than they want to go. They take the easier road and sell a "death" benefit.

When an Investment Advisor is asked about life insurance, they seldom know the various applications available for their clients. While they may believe they know what they are doing, it has been my experience that most don't. I have witnessed so many instances that even the people they turn to for help, the 'home office' experts, have little expertise themselves, the kind of which they need to help their own advisors.

Keep in mind that a good life insurance agent can help you with the best solutions available for you, in your particular situation. The ideas presented here represent a few of the many. Taxes too, can play a big part in the uses for life insurance and you should at a minimum, have a tax consultant, preferably a Certified Public Accountant review any decision you make. Especially true if there is a potential tax scenario to any actions that may be undertook.

The first thing you have to do is find the 'right' life insurance agent. Preferably the agent will have at least a few years of experience with a Mutual Life Insurance Company. This is not to say that a new agent can't help you, but in my view, I prefer an agent with product knowledge and experience.

I strongly urge you to use only a Mutual life insurance company, and one that's been around for at least a hundred years. Publicly traded life insurance companies have stockholders to account for. Guess where their gains have to go.

Dividends which I think of as policy owner gains, come primarily from three sources,

1) Mortality expense, the better the underwriting, the better the exposure

2) Administrative expenses, the lower the cost, the better return on the dollar

3) Investment results, the longer, the stronger returns benefit the policy owner.

I like a long track record when it comes to dividends and financial strength. There's comfort in consistency. Why is that important to you? Because it's your money we're talking about.

You've heard about other products that are 'safe' with great growth opportunities. They all sound good and I especially like the line for one product, "You can't lose your money in an Indexed Universal Life policy." Want to bet! Nearly all products tied into the market are situational. There are negative effects from late payments, no payments, stretched out 'bear' markets, and whether or not a client needs use of that money.

When working with agents you know, but who sell products other than whole life with a mutual insurance company, don't lose sight here.

Only participating guaranteed whole life insurance policies and their limited pay options, will keep growing,

- ✓ Guaranteed cash values keep growing
- ✓ Can grow even if you don't pay premiums
- ✓ Can grow even if you create or have a loan
- ✓ Grows even if security markets are falling
- ✓ Mutual Company is not publicly traded, no stock owners
- ✓ Participate in the gains of the Insurance Company, you are a shareholder
- ✓ Guaranteed Life Insurance Amount
- ✓ Level lifetime premiums (or shorter) guaranteed
- ✓ Creditor proof in the majority of states
- ✓ No policy owner who has maintained their policies has ever lost a penny
- ✓ Nearly 200 years of consistent, successful experience with these products

Universal Life, Variable Universal Life, and Indexed Life Insurance policies have a surprise for most policy owners at some point down the road. They leave the door open and clients can almost count on receiving a letter that says one or all of these,

- ✓ "You can keep your insurance, but the new (higher) premium is."
- ✓ "You can continue the same premium, but to keep an amount of life insurance you have, the face amount will drop to....."
- ✓ Can (hopefully) take a reduced 'paid-up' amount of coverage.

If an agent marketing those products says that can't happen, ask him/her to put it in writing. Let them know the letter will go to the insurance company for verification. You don't need propaganda here. It's your money and you have the right to know the framework your policy is structured into.

In most interest bearing 'type' insurance contracts, the insurance carrier maintains the right to move the mortality table to a more expensive item charge. This by itself can cripple many illustrations shown to the public. The carrier can also change the interest on Universal life contracts and/or the so-called cap on Indexed type contracts.

Under the right circumstances however, such as higher premiums per thousand, these policies can be effectively used, but maintenance runs high.

I also have a litmus test. I run a 10-pay life insurance illustration (pay 10 years only) and in the 14th year I withdraw 'all' the premiums paid during those ten pay years. I put the same numbers into an indexed universal life policy for comparison. Since I mentioned this, you can guess at the results. Most interest-bearing policies will lapse, and generally, that's not true of the mutual insurance company.

Note that almost all the IUL policy illustrations show positive numbers in the market every year. They give a lot of reasons for justification, but check out what happens if there is a loss in one of every five years. There are also limitations and restrictions in those contracts that client's should understand. By the way, according to some industry sources, the market usually decreases once in every four years on average.

Another surprise is when those holding these IUL contracts are notified and embedded in a letter, that the insurance company has increased the mortality cost inside your policy. Yes, they can change the cost of insurance and the rules for earning interest. Insurance company wins, policy owner loses.

Since this seems like a good moment to air a complaint out I will, and this one goes against the insurance commissioners in each state. Knowing these policies put the policy owner at risk, they let insurance companies call them permanent. Really! If they were permanent, that would put the insurance company at risk, not the client.

That is baloney on their part, and when agents sell those contracts at lower than necessary lifetime premiums, policy owners will suffer down the road. With these policies, the insurance companies change the rules and the policies start blowing apart when clients are in their late sixties and beyond.

Great timing, and did I mention how the states collect taxes on insurance premiums. That's right, many states collect anywhere from 1% to 2% of your premium payments every year. In some states this tax is up to 2.5% of all taxes collected by the states. Just another little tax that you can't see. Don't you just love politicians? I digress.

Now, after you've found the agent and the mutual life insurance company you want, you need to make some decisions with the help of your agent and these are key,

- ✓ Determine how much money you want available and when, then target that date. The premiums are then a function of your targeted 'savings.'
- ✓ How much insurance is needed?
- ✓ How to maximize your premium dollars for savings and family protection.

The amount of insurance needed varies among clients, even those with what would seem to be similar situations. A good agent will not only help you with your decision, the agent will know how to structure the policy with your best interests in mind.

Think about the amount of money you want in your 'tank.' If it's $50,000 in ten years, then you should target the payments required for the next ten years. One easy method is to divide the amount desired by the number of years until you reach your target date. Keep in mind that these payments can be off-set and/or reduced by the amount of financing savings you have when using the policy's cash values.

That said, remember that you don't have to wait ten years to start using it. Using certain policies allows you to start as soon as the first-year premiums are made. So, you can start saving financed 'interest costs' quickly and that will also offset the premiums. It's your money, make it work for you.

That may seem like a daunting task up front, but do put your life insurance agent to work by having the agent assist you. In the first few years, some people will have to tighten their 'budget.' However, in just a few years and for the rest of their lives, they will be in a much better financial situation than they are now in, and that will be true every year for the rest of their life.

In your meeting with the agent you choose, be open and let the agent know what you want to do and ask for direction. Be sure to share the information requested including, the current amount of debt, how much you overall, your monthly payments, their duration, and the amount or percentage that is going to interest. Like a good doctor, they need to know all the moving parts before prescribing a remedy.

At this point or after doing a review, the agent will also point out the most strategic procedures for you to follow. You might be told to pay off, using your insurance, the debt with the smallest amount due on it. Then using those dollars, you were paying to help with the insurance and using it all to move on to the next smallest debt payment. It's a process that will work and clear up your debts faster than many other methods.

The agent will take an application on your life and you may need a physical. You will have to give thorough answers on your medical history. In addition to your completing this part, the insurance company will verify or seek additional information from your doctors. They will check on other items as well such as dangerous activities like skydiving. Fortunately, today this underwriting process is much quicker and more accurate today.

When everything is completed, the agent will come back, present your policy, review it with you, and answer your questions, but it shouldn't stop there. Ask how much will be available to you in the first year and projections going forward.

You want the ability to use your insurance quickly, to shed some of the interest you are currently paying, remembering that the agent is part of your team. Make sure you understand the policy basics and what you are doing. The results will be based on what you do know and the procedures you will follow.

If you feel like certain things in the policy are above your head, that's fine. You just became the average American. However, there are certain key points you should know at the time of purchase or during reviews including,

    a) The loan interest rate
    b) The Premiums, annually and/or monthly
    c) The Total Cash Values in force
    d) The Total Cash Values projected
    e) The Total Death Benefit including dividend additions.

Walking away with that information will put you ahead of your peers. It's also critical in those moments when you may have the need to know that information and the agent isn't available.

There are many key reasons why you should be reviewing your life insurance frequently. For myself, I like to tell my clients that **it is your money, you want to stay in touch with it** and you want to know your options.

Chapter 9

FINAL THOUGHTS

> **"The Best Way to Predict the Future,**
> **is to Create it."**
> *Peter Drucker*

Common sense tells us that the life insurance death benefit is 'incidental' to one's greatest need for money, the need for financing. When we understand the importance for funding and the cost of that financing, then the importance of life insurance hits us over the head.

Life insurance is used to protect those we love and care about. While the death benefit is important and the reason most people purchase life insurance, the magnitude of that insurance becomes significantly higher when people learn it can also help to help us achieve a better lifestyle. As if that weren't enough, it provides supplemental retirement income during retirement and protects us from creditors.

Life insurance isn't just a product. It's an immensely important product. For those of us who have responsibilities, it comes only after food, clothing, and shelter, and it's there for us to use the entirety of our lives.

It's always easy to say, "All you have to do to get started is just do it," but that's not real life. People tell me they are working all day and don't have time to do this 'stuff.' Then there's the jam-packed weekend they've been looking forward to spending with their families.

The younger you are, the more likelihood that you've got things to do with your children. As you grow older, there are family gatherings, ball games to watch and parties to attend. The older you get, those in retirement, the more important it is to spend time talking with other retirees, solving the world's problems today only to wake up tomorrow morning and have to start all over again. This too I know, takes effort, and has proven to be tiring.

Time is important. I realize how precious it really is. Try raising nine children and suddenly nearly two dozen grandchildren. Yes, time is precious, but the real question you have to ask yourself is, what your priorities are.

However, this is an investment in time. Think about it, if you can save $400 or $600 a month in interest payments every month, how much more fun would your free time be? Let's say your life insurance can save you $500 every month, that's $6,000, that's $6,000 every year. Over ten years you saved $60,000. Isn't spending an hour or two every year reviewing your financial plan with your advisor worth the effort?

What! You don't have a plan. Well you do, even if you never thought about one. It's called a Default Financial Plan. It's the one without a road map. If you get to where you would like to be, that's wonderful, although it's an accident.

Would you get on an airplane to fly from Philadelphia to Atlanta without a pilot? Of course, you wouldn't, and you shouldn't try to map a financial course without a good advisor, at least not if you have a destination in mind, or maybe even safety.

If you can throw away hundreds of thousands of dollars because you aren't interested in checking out concepts that are 'foreign' to you, that's a mistake. Imagine if you are a parent and fail to share these ideas with your adult children. You have to take the time and get out of the box you are in. We all have to, from time to time, get out of our box.

A few of those who are older might say that this idea doesn't work for them. Nothing could be further from the truth as you have already seen. Not only will this idea work for you, but you will be passing wealth down to your children or grandchildren without much effort. They will notice the difference, and it will impact them every month of their life.

Then there are those who think they are uninsurable and this couldn't possibly work for them. I don't care if you are highly rated for life insurance or even uninsurable as some of us are. This model works for you as well as for any retiree.

If there is any real problem with starting this program, it's in one's head. We have been operated on, sliced and diced, with an implant that says whole life insurance is a bad buy. Those who have argued that point, are clueless.

Next time someone says that to you, smile inwardly and know that you are wiser than the one making that statement.

On the other side of the table is the 'real' you. You have to want to improve your position. To improve your financial balance sheet. It is that desire and the passion you show for it that will make or break you. To increase your usable wealth while getting out of debt is something you can do. The only obstacle in front of you, is you.

You can either be a slave to money or it's master. The choice is up to you. The ideas you are seeing are solid and extremely beneficial to both you while alive and to your heirs when that time comes. The focus for this discussion is money, are the benefits of money are contained in the life insurance you purchase for your family.

While it is quite easy to get started building your own finance company, that is creating your own capital, it is another thing to know how to do it. That's where a good agent comes into play.

I hope I've put the ideas of un-insurability and age to rest. "An Investment in knowledge pays the best interest," Ben Franklin said. I believe that once you mentally process this program, you will want more guaranteed cash value life insurance than you ever imagined.

If you hadn't known it before, I hop you've recognized it by now, one of our greatest needs in life is financing, we use it every year in one way or another. I have seen budgets that include financing payments for homes, cars, televisions, vacations, credit cards and personal loans. As I have repeatedly stressed, when the interest on all your invoices are added together, that becomes more than just an intriguing number. When you add up all the interest on each item, then multiply it by twelve months, the numbers are overwhelming.

When the saver puts down the amount of interest 'lost' on every dollar spent over a given period that number is just as overwhelming. Again, a saver who uses savings to make purchases loses more than another person who uses credit. They both lose. Run the numbers!

Both a borrower and a saver purchase a $30,000 car. The borrower gets 8% interest payments (if lower, the spread you see here will be greater yet) over 5 years. The cost for the five years is $36,498

The saver makes 5% on his investments and spends the $30,000 that was previously saved. The $30,000 would have grown to $38,288 and it would have continued its growth beyond this point. The difference of $1,790 favors the borrower. The saver would have been better off borrowing the money for the car.

Finance companies and banks are successful because their profits are generated with your savings at low interest rates, and they in turn lend it out at much higher rates, maybe even back to you. It is fortunate for some that they are there. It's not fortunate for you if you have been reading this book. You should understand what is happening.

Let's see what you want your money to do. Utilizing a strategy to accumulate an increasing pool of money with accessibility, control, and uninterrupted compounding. The following advantages are standard for people using guaranteed cash value life insurance. This time with a little more detail.

Think about it, Life Insurance Advantages

1) All contributions to the guaranteed cash value life insurance policy are dollars taken from one of our pockets and put into our other pocket. The money is yours, the same as if it were in a bank. Only this is "**Money with Benefits**."

2) Growth is guaranteed in 'up' stock markets, it is guaranteed in 'down' stock markets. Bonds may go up and down, but cash values are steady climbers in all weather conditions.

3) It is safe and it is liquid. During the Great Depression, not one person lost a single penny with their guaranteed life insurance policies, not one penny ever.

4) You want your money to grow income tax-free. You are willing to take a small hit on the rate of return because there are no taxes to pay while your money grows. It can be a great replacement for bonds. That is just one element of life insurance and important to you. Not only that, it is not even reportable to the IRS at this point.

5) The returns look very good when using a life insurance policy for self-funding purchases.

6) Distributions made using the 'loan' provision are not taxable. Loans are more beneficial because the death benefit is reduced dollar for dollar with the loan. The total cash values are growing faster than the interest on a loan. In essence, you are earning money on your loan than if you made straight withdrawals. Where else can you do that?

7) When making a loan, the cash values are still there. You are borrowing from the insurance company against your equity in the contract. It is a 'fully' collateralized loan. The earnings on your cash value are generally greater than the loan interest that is contractually due on the policy. No other liquid asset that I am aware of, <u>rewards you for borrowing money.</u>

8) The cash availability is guaranteed in the contract. There are no credit forms or credit checks to be completed and no reasons for the loan have to be given. Simply ask for the money.

9) At your death, any outstanding loans are automatically paid from the proceeds of your contract. If you borrowed from any other source, that loan would be due at your death and the proceeds of the life insurance would more than likely be used. Same required payment, only a simpler step when using the money in the life insurance policy.

10) If for some reason, you need or want a 'bank' loan, the cash values in your policy are outstanding collateral to other lenders. They know it's as good as cash, as solid to them as if it were in a bank.

11) Policy loan Payments are unstructured until you decide what you want to do and how you are going to do it. You may want to wait a few months before you start your pay-back, or pay partially on the loan for a period of time. You set your own terms. However, it is preferable, especially if you pay back what you would have paid a lender. Repeatedly, you are creating your own wealth.

12) One option is to use the dividends to make the interest payments internally. Your policy is continues growing but subsequently the

values are reduced by the amount of interest covered by the dividends. Still, you would have saved the interest payment and there would be no loan against the cash values.

13) Loans are private. A loan will not show up anywhere else. This is a great advantage for you since it will not count against your credit score. You are building a good credit history and maintaining a high credit score can have a dramatic impact on your life.

14) Investments, especially real estate can be noticeably enhanced when using your life insurance cash values. Both the real estate, with a mortgage and the policy with a loan, continue to grow (in the case of real estate, it should) and then you would have positive rates of return on both sides of the ledger. That is double dollar returns, doubling your pleasure. This money can stretch in any direction you choose.

15) Seeking more retirement income. All advisors at times hear clients who want to put more money into qualified accounts such as an IRA or their 401(k) at work, but are restricted by regulations. Imagine that! Life insurance, other than underwriting restrictions, has no such stipulations on how much you can purchase.

16) Death benefits are income tax-free and most states do not apply an inheritance tax to the insurance when it goes to a named beneficiary. Another nice win for the life insurance contract, saving you even more money.

17) When you purchase a guaranteed, participating life insurance policy, the insurance company takes the risk. The premium, the face amount, and the cash values are guaranteed. This is not true in policies that are interest adjusted for premiums, cash values, and death benefits.

People use banks because they want safety and liquidity. They don't mind getting a smaller return on their money, but like Will Rogers, they just want their money back. The guaranteed cash value life insurance does much more than just give you your money back, much more.

If there is a concern for the financial stability of the mutual life insurance companies, there shouldn't be. There is unmatched strength among the mutual life insurance companies. With a history going back nearly 200 years, the mutual life companies have been safe. No one has lost money with these companies. In fact, those who were able to salvage money, and didn't put it under their pillows, put it in the life insurance companies.

Those during the Great Depression that were able to salvage money, and didn't put it under their pillows, put it into life insurance contracts.

Policy-owners have received dividends every year. Policy-owners are the 'shareholders' of the company and they are the ones who profit by a successful insurance company. Not outside investors. You have to remember that the company gains come from better mortality, lowering expenses and investments.

NOTES

Notes, clarifications, disclaimers

✓ **Annuities** are not a favorite of mine. Primary feature is the guaranteed lifetime income that you can't outlive. However, there are items that should be kept in mind. For instance, if the payout is 5% for life and inflation grows at 3%, it takes 32 years to break even. That is, to receive back the full current value of a dollar. As for legacies to heirs, most annuities will have zero inheritance values after the 22nd year. Still, there are valuable applications where annuities work for some.

✓ **Bankruptcies**, most states will give creditor proof protection to life insurance cash values in full or in part. You should know what your state provides.

✓ **Bank Savings Accounts** are interest-bearing deposit accounts held at a bank or other financial institution that pays interest at a 'prudent' rate. They also may charge fees unless you maintain a certain average monthly balance in the account.

✓ **BOLI**, signifies <u>Bank Owned Life Insurance</u> or <u>Business Owned Life Insurance</u>. The bank is the payer, owner, and beneficiary of a life insurance policy purchased on employees. These policies are used as a tax shelter for the financial institutions, which in turn does leverage its tax-free savings provisions as funding mechanisms for employee benefits as well as other uses such as when deemed as good positive leverage.

✓ **Calculations** in this book were performed using Excel, Bankrate.com and life insurance illustrations from different mutual life insurance companies.

✓ **Cash Values** are guaranteed by the life insurance company and depend on the financial strength of the company. Most states have a "Guarantee Association" of life insurance companies licensed and doing business in the state. The Pennsylvania Association guarantees up to $300,000 per contract on the guaranteed cash values.

- ✓ **Credit Card Companies** make the bulk of their money from three things: interest, fees charged to card holders, and transaction fees paid by businesses that accept credit cards.

- ✓ **Dividends**, in illustrations are neither guarantees nor estimates of the future, but are based on current dividend scales. Over time they play a significant part in the returns on a life insurance policy. It's important to point out that the mutual insurance companies I have worked with, have never failed to pay a dividend. This has been true for more than 170 years with my primary companies. Dividends used to purchase paid-up additions change the dividends into their own guaranteed cash values. Thus, once additional coverage is purchased, that coverage has cash values.

- ✓ **Favorite Life Insurance Companies** include in alphabetical order, Guardian, MassMutual, New York Life, Northwestern Mutual, and Penn Mutual. There are a few others as well, but only a few.

- ✓ **Fifth Dividend Option** is a whole life dividend option in which a portion of the dividends paid are used to purchase one-year term insurance equal to the policy's current cash value. The total death proceeds would be equal to the face amount of the policy, plus dividend additions, plus the cash values in the policy less any loans.

- ✓ **Individual Retirement Plans** (IRA) are tax-advantaged accounts designed to help you save for retirement.

- ✓ **Mutual Life Insurance Companies** are insurance companies owned entirely by its policyholders. Any gains made by a mutual insurance company are retained within the company or distributed to policyholders. This may generally take the form of the purchase of dividend additions, dividend distributions or reduced future premiums.

- ✓ **Non-Qualified Retirement Plans** are tax-deferred, employer-sponsored retirement plans that can and do fall outside of the employee retirement income security act (ERISA) guidelines. Non-qualified plans are designed to meet specialized retirement needs for key executives and other select employees.

- ✓ **Parties to a Contract**
  - o The Insured
  - o The Payer

- o The Owner
- o The Beneficiary

✓ **Repetitions** were used for those points that I felt needed to be stressed.

✓ **Split-Dollar** There are a wide variety of uses for split-dollar plans today. Split-dollar involves two or more people or entities splitting the costs and/or benefits of permanent life insurance. It is an outstanding benefit when used by knowledgeable agents. It satisfies many needs and wishes at one time. It has historically been used as a business employee benefit program, but it can be used in a multiple number of ways, including additional ways to benefit one's family.

✓ **Tax-Qualified Retirement Plans** are employer-sponsored retirement plan that qualifies for special tax treatment under Section 401(a) of the Internal Revenue Code. To separate tax-sheltered IRA's from non-qualified plans, I have lumped them into this area.

**The secret to getting ahead,
Is getting started
Mark Twain**

www.ingramcontent.com/pod-product-compliance
Lightning Source LLC
Chambersburg PA
CBHW081725220526
45468CB00008B/1977